FOG BELLS

First published in 2025 by
The Dedalus Press
13 Moyclare Road
Baldoyle
Dublin D13 K1C2
Ireland

www.**dedaluspress**.com

ISBN 9781915629333 (paperback)
ISBN 9781915629326 (hardback)

Dedalus Press titles are available in Ireland
from Argosy Books (www.argosybooks.ie) and in the UK
from Inpress Books (www.inpressbooks.co.uk).

Cover image by Salma Caller,
www.salmaahmadcaller.com,
by kind permission of the artist.

The Dedalus Press receives financial assistance from
The Arts Council / An Chomhairle Ealaíon.

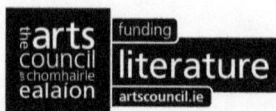

the arts council chomhairle ealaíon

funding literature
artscouncil.ie

FOG BELLS

8 Contemporary Turkish Poets

Translated, with an Introduction,
by NEIL P. DOHERTY

DEDALUS PRESS

ACKNOWLEDGEMENTS AND THANKS

I owe much to my readers in various parts of the globe who read the manuscript over the past eighteen months and provided many invaluable suggestions and a great deal of support and encouragement. So *teşekkürler*/thanks to Spencer Burke, Barış Celiloğlu, Gökçenur Çelebioğlu, Declan Drohan, Trevor Joyce, Jeffrey Kahrs, Mel Kenne, Derick Mattern, Gonca Özmen and John W. Sexton.

Special thanks to Salma Caller for the cover art and for reading sections of the manuscript over the past year.

Many thanks to to Pat Boran of Dedalus Press for taking on this project at a time when it seems the world is growing smaller and more insular.

Versions of some of these poems have appeared in the following journals: *The Antonym, Cyphers, The Jolt, Modern Poetry in Translation, Púca* and *Versopolis*.

***

The publisher would like to thank the individual poets for granting permission to publish their original Turkish language poems alongside the English translations in this anthology.

To my mother, father, sisters and my daughter Aoibhinn
in whom the two rivers flow.

Contents

≈

Cevat Çapan

≈

Mehmet Taner

≈

Lale Müldür

≈

Mustafa Köz

Elif Sofya

Birhan Keskin

~

Gökçenur Ç.

⌒

Gonca Özmen

⌒

INTRODUCTION

⌇

The book you hold in your hands may best be imagined as a small section of a much larger tapestry. One that could only be presented in all its colour and depth by means of a sprawling multivolume work covering, for instance, the poetry of the late Ottoman Empire, the search for new poetics and verse forms during the early years of the Republic, the re-emergence of folk poetry, the various modernist movements that later shook the tradition down to its core, the persistence of political verse, be it socialist or Islamic, and the spectacular rise in the quality and quantity of poetry written by women. Representing all of these is beyond the scope of this book and the ability of any single translator. Instead, this volume offers a generous selection of the work of eight living Turkish poets in order to give the reader an insight into the depth and richness of contemporary poetry in the Turkish language and also to showcase the different voices and styles that each poet has tried out over the course of their writing lives.

Often poetry from languages such as Turkish become trapped in an arid wasteland that Hamad Dabashi styles as, "area studies"[1] In other words, the poetry is not seen as poetry, but rather as a series of curios displayed in some exotic Wunderkammer to be poured over as sociological tracts rather than read as literature. One of the principle aims of this book is to present these poets as poets, each of whom has a deep awareness of both the Turkish tradition and current world poetry.

In writing an introduction to any anthology from what might be termed an under-translated language, the translator is aware that the reader will come to these poets knowing nothing of the tradition in which they write. Being Irish, I might imagine an anthology of contemporary Irish poetry in English (Irish language poetry is a case closer to Turkish in some ways) set before readers who know nothing of Yeats, Clarke, Kavanagh, Boland or Kinsella. Yet this is what faces any translator of Turkish poetry. Were one to ask any poet or poetry reader in Ireland, or any other European country, to name a Turkish poet, chances are that most would struggle to name a single one.

Yet Turkey is a country that prides itself on its poets. Indeed, it wouldn't be too much of an exaggeration to claim that poetry is an essential node of Turkish life: students copy the passionately erotic poems of Cemal Süreya into their notebooks; leftists quote lines by Nâzım Hikmet over *rakı;* protestors scrawl verses from the radical poets of the Second New Movement on walls and pavements while fleeing from the police; the poems of Gülten Akın are read aloud and shared in university dormitories; and some reverently quote to one another long sections of the work of Sezai Karakoç. Many poems are set to music and sung in cafés and the streets. During the Gezi Uprising of 2013 the protestors set up a library in Gezi Park and stocked it with the work of poets like Edip Cansever, Behçet Necatigil, Didem Madak and Orhan Veli. Yet, outside the country one might well claim that Turkish poetry does not exist, that it is invisible. And one might well ask why this is so.

An American poet friend once suggested that the reason Turkish poetry was so little known in the West was merely because there were very few translators translating the work into English. However, this has never been the case. Over the past seventy years or so several translators, such as Talat S. Halman, Nermin Menemencioğlu, Saliha Paker, Feyyaz Kayacan Fergar, Mel Kenne, Murat Nemet-Nejat, Cliff and Selhan Endres, George Messo, Buğra Giritlioğlu, Jeffrey Kahrs, Mete Özel, Derick Mattern, Gökçenur Ç., Suat Karantay, Donny Smith, Richard and Julia Tillinghast, Ruth Christie and Richard McKane have worked tirelessly to bring Turkish poetry to readers of English. Despite the excellence of their work, it is still a fact that the poetry lacks the visibility (and prestige) of poetry translated from Greek, Polish or Spanish. Very few Turkish poets are published in single author collections and precious few anthologies have been published over the past thirty years. While the market is flooded with a glut of Neruda and Rilke translations, major Turkish figures such as Turgut Uyar, Didem Madak, küçük İskender and İsmet Özel are represented in English by a few stray translations in old anthologies or on pages tucked away in obscure corners of the internet. Might there be a deeper reason for this neglect of what Murat Nemet-Nejat has called "one of the major poetry traditions" of the modern era? [2]

In the late nineteenth century certain factors came together in a way that subsequently allowed poets in the Turkish language to forge a poetry of great originality and substance. The first of these was the dual tradition of divan and folk poetry. The former being the verse of the Ottoman court written in a form of Turkish heavily influenced by both Arabic and Persian, the latter composed in a language mostly free of foreign influence and sung across Anatolia by troubadour like poets called *aşık* (those who are in love). The folk tradition was a storehouse of riddles, rhymes, laments, satires and love lyrics which often contained an explicit or implicit erotic theme [3]. Divan poetry, in contrast, written in what was essentially an artificial dialect, took delight in multilingual puns, and what might be called codes that were intended for a very select audience. While these two traditions were distinct and, for most of their long history, kept their distance from one another, they both contain a large number of poems that can be read both as thrilling love poetry and/or as passionate entreaties to a capricious God. The fact that Turkish has no grammatical gender leaves these poems suspended in a delicious state of uncertainty. The lover yearns to melt into the presence of the beloved, who is never named, never imprisoned within a single identity.

The second great influence on the development of modern Turkish poetics was its encounter with French poetry. Throughout the long nineteenth century Turkish poets began to read and translate French, and poets such as Baudelaire, Verlaine,

Lamartine and Hugo became bywords for a new kind of modern poetry, one that had little to do with the native traditions. It might well be claimed that the encounter with French poetry spurred Turkish poets to take poetry down to the teeming streets of their cities in order to capture sounds and smells that had hitherto been foreign to their tradition. This interest in the poetry of another language and culture was merely the first step in a long process that witnessed the translation into Turkish of a huge number of world classics. It must be noted that many of the poets in this volume are also translators who have added a number of vital translations of both poetry and prose to the ever-expanding corpus of translated literature in Turkish.

The last, and possibly saddest, influence is an extra-literary one. For much of the last one hundred-and-fifty years Turkey, first as the Ottoman State and then as its successor, the Turkish Republic, has been politically, and even in certain ways, culturally unstable. The trauma connected to the collapse of the Empire is something that has yet to be fully grasped and its repercussions are felt to this day across the region, from the Balkans to Palestine and from Iraq to Egypt. Many of the old certainties were swept away: dress, customs, architecture, the place of religion, family structures, eating habits, and even time itself were changed in a series of what some have called Westernizing reforms that left children unable to understand the world of their parents.

One of the most radical was that of language. Over the course of just six months the government of Mustafa Kemal Atatürk did away with the old Ottoman script, the Perso-Arabic writing system that had been in use for some seven hundred years. Yet this was merely the first step in a process that aimed to purify the language and rid it of Persian and Arabic elements.

Throughout these periods of chaos poets wrote, sometimes in support of the new world and sometimes against it, but striving, all the while, to make sense of it. Readers turned to poetry in the uncertainty that surrounded them, hoping to find something that would, at least, offer some kind of shelter amid the storm of change. At best, like fog bells, the poems gathered here might even guide them toward a safer shore. But the question remains, why have these bells, which over the course of almost one hundred years have rung out so clearly in Turkish, been for the most part ignored in the West?

Perhaps an essay written by one Joseph Brodsky might help us unravel this knot[(4)]. In 1984 Brodsky visited Istanbul to keep a promise he had made himself on leaving the Soviet Union to 'circumnavigate the inhabited world along the latitude and along the longitude on which Leningrad is situated'. While Istanbul lies some eight degrees west of the meridian in question, this erstwhile citizen of the Third Rome, and lover of the First, decided to visit the Second. His time in Istanbul is recorded in an essay which exists in two different versions, one written in his native Russian entitled simply 'Journey to Istanbul' and a second translated by the poet with Alan Myers bearing the deliberately anti-Yeatsian title of 'Flight from Byzantium'. From the outset Brodsky makes it clear that there was nothing in the modern polis of 'miracle, bird or golden handiwork' and the sea was not 'dolphin-torn' or 'gong-tormented', merely run down, dated and cheap. Indeed, one of the main tropes that runs through the essay is the idea that everything in Istanbul is irrelevant, that history has side-stepped the city, leaving it wallowing in eastern indolence and dirt. Everything in the city makes the visitor feel like they're moving in the wrong direction, away from the light and back into darkness. The Turkish populace is to be found in "a state of total stupor whiling its time away in squalid snack bars, tilting its heads as in a *namaz* (ritual prayer) in reverse toward the television screen, where somebody is permanently beating somebody else up". Everything in the city is described as shabby and third-rate. This even applies to those great monuments of Ottoman Istanbul, the imperial mosques, denigrated by Brodsky as "enormous toads in frozen stone, squatting on the earth, unable to stir". The squatting, shitting temples are mired in their own muck. How could one expect such a people, burdened as they are with such notions of art, content as they are to dwell in their crumbling and filthy city, to write poetry? The idea simply does not, will not cross Brodsky's mind. Turks are shoeshine boys or despots. They while their lives away, tea-glass in hand. Brodsky then goes on to condense the entire poetic history of one of the oldest cities in the world into the three years Constantine Cavafy spent there.[5] Cavafy, Brodsky's ideal Cavafy – though not the real Kavafis of Alexandria – is all of the Polis that is of any interest to Brodsky. In an essay dealing with this, the poet and critic Necmi Zekâ, wonders: "why such a well-read poet had shown no interest at all in the poetry of a country which prides herself about producing many world-class poets?" But how could he have had an interest in something that he couldn't imagine? Would it be too much to suggest that poetry in this language, poetry written by these people was simply something Brodsky could not conceive of? [6]

One might counter and say that this is simply the view of one poet. Yet there has been, since the time of E.J.W. Gibb, the Scottish translator of Ottoman poetry who viewed the tradition as a poor imitation of Persian poetry, a noticeable lack of interest in poetry written in Turkish. While various historical factors have brought other poetries to the fore, one could mention here how the collapse of the Eastern Bloc had many Anglophone poets tripping over themselves in a rush to 'translate' Hungarian, Polish and Czech poetry, and the inhumane oppression of the Palestinian people has brought certain poets from that country to an international readership, Turkish poetry seems to have been overlooked and ignored. One wonders if some lingering view of 'the Turk' as the historical other, the antithesis of civilization and order, has something to do with this? Or, as Orhan Pamuk has elsewhere asked, are Westerners only interested in a literature like Turkish when it is loaded with local colour or if they feel it will offer some insight into the politics of the country or, even worse, into something as dubious as the 'Turkish soul'? As he remarked: "When I write about love, the critics in the US and Britain say that this Turkish writer writes very interesting things about Turkish love. Why can't love be general? I am always resentful and angry of this attempt to narrow me and my capacity to experience this humanity. You are squeezed and narrowed down, cornered down as a writer whose book is considered only the representation of his national voice and a little bit of anthropological curiosity."[7] So here, in this volume, are poems presented simply as poems, not as sociological texts or exotica. These poets cannot be narrowed down to any one thing, for, to paraphrase Whitman, they contain, as all good poets in every language do, multitudes.

The most contentious aspect of any anthology is, without doubt, that of selection. As was highlighted above, this volume is not a definitive anthology of Turkish poetry, it is more of a sampler of the riches the language contains. Many, many fine poets were excluded and I can safely say that the current Turkish poetry scene could yield several samplers of this nature to complement the one you are currently reading. The selection for this volume has been made from living poets. The oldest poet in the book, Cevat Çapan, was born in 1933 and the youngest, Gonca Özmen, in 1982. It might very well be claimed that, between these two dates, Turkish poetry emerged from the Ottoman past and grew into, what Mel Kenne has called, "one of the richest and yet least known veins of literary ore in the world". [8] It did this by dint of a number of movements, such as *Garip*/Strange, which began in the 1930s and '40s and the *İkinci Yeni*/Second New of the 1950s and '60s, that, by drawing on native examples from both the divan and folk traditions and such western movements as surrealism and cubism, turned poetry on its head. One must also mention the importance of figures such as Nazım Hikmet, for many years the only widely translated Turkish poet, and Behçet Necatigil who synthesised elements of the Ottoman past with high modernism, who were never really part of any movement.

While making the selection I chose poets I felt represented, in different ways, the fruit of all these changes. I also chose those I believe I have been able to translate successfully into English. Any anthology built around poets from similar backgrounds and/or poetic movements runs the risk of sounding like a series of voices that are almost impossible to distinguish clearly. One of the aims of this volume has to been to give space to poets who have created their own poetic worlds to let them sing in both harmony and discord. The attentive reader will note that, though each voice is distinct, there are echoes that reverberate between the voyages of Cevat Çapan and the intense, riddling music of Gonca Özmen, for instance, between the gnostic ruminations of Lale Müldür and the political concerns of Mustafa Köz, between the ecopoetics of Elif Sofya and mysterious narratives of Mehmet Taner, between the haunting laments of Birhan Keskin and the playful seriousness of Gökçenur Ç. that suggest a tradition that is both in dialogue with itself and also keen to seek new, unexplored paths of expression. In addition, I have sought to present poets who have previously been translated alongside some who have never before appeared in English.

As Andrei Codrescu has said of the translation of Romanian poetry, the ideal reader, after encountering the work of Lucian Blaga, should feel the need to learn Romanian.[9] One can only hope that this book might urge a handful of readers to become curious about the Turkish language and the treasures it holds. These fog bells, which were first sounded at one edge of the European land mass, are now ringing out at its opposite extremity. Who knows what new routes, what hitherto unexplored songlines they may inspire?

A NOTE ON THE TURKISH LANGUAGE AND TRANSLATION

The Turkish language is a member of the Oghuz branch of the Turkic family. It was once believed that the Turkic family was a part of a greater Altaic language family that included such languages as Japanese, Korean and Mongolian. However, linguists no longer believe this to be the case, and the Turkic languages are thought to be unrelated to any other language family. The reason these languages were once grouped together is because they share some salient features, namely: agglutination, vowel harmony and lack of grammatical gender. Indeed, in the nineteenth century some linguists linked Turkish to Hungarian and Finnish as these two languages also share these features. While these theories are now discredited, the fact remains that Turkish is unrelated to any Indo-European language and, therefore, has nothing in common with any of them. It possesses a very free syntax, which allows poets to change the place of words in a poetic line in a way that is almost impossible in English. As an agglutinative language, it constructs long, complex sentences from single roots. If we take the word *ev*, 'house', we can start to build meaning by adding suffixes:

> *Ev*, house
> *Ev-ler*, hous*es*
> *Ev-ler-den*, from the hous*es*
> *Ev-ler-den-miş*, apparently from the hous*es*

Allowing the speaker to change, with a single suffix, the meaning and feeling of any word constitutes the real richness of the language, one that poses a difficulty for any translator. In the hands of an capable poet it is a medium which can express a thought or emotion in the most concise manner, often with as little as one or two words, one that may often take the more ponderous English language a whole sentence, or long poetic line, to convey. The language also possesses a rich storehouse of tenses, including one that is used to comment or report on events which one has not personally witnessed or which one wants to distance oneself from – the *miş* noted above. Added to that, Turkish has no grammatical gender, so nouns are not marked as masculine, feminine or neutral as in most Indo-European languages. Moreover, the language has but a single pronoun, *o*, which is used for *he*, *she* and *it*. This offers a poet huge scope to play with ideas of gender and identity. The reader may never know if the subject of any poem is male, female or non-binary. The language arrived at state of gender neutrality thousands of years before it became an issue in the West. Turkish is concise, fluid, and elegant, capable of quick shifts in tone and subtle shades of meaning. The task of the translator is to try to capture these without slavishly hewing to any single philosophy of translation. Each poem asks the translator to re-examine their working methods to find the best possible way of carrying Turkish modes of expression into English, all while making the translations work as poems yet without obscuring from the reader that these texts were initially written in a language utterly different from their native tongue. In some of the translations I have used Hiberno-English forms and idioms simply because it is my first language and because the poems seemed to need something different from the standard British and/or American Englishes that dominate Anglophone translation.

—Neil P. Doherty
Üsküdar, İstanbul, August 2025

REFERENCES

1. Dabashi, H. (2015). *Can Non-Europeans Think?* Bloomsbury.
2. Nemet-Nejat, M. (trans./ed.) (2004). *Eda: An Anthology of Contemporary Turkish Poetry.* Talisman House.
3. Roberts, C. (2020, June 22). "Poetry Gives a Voice to the Voiceless": An Interview with Gonca Özmen. A New Divan. A Lyrical Dialogue Between East & West. https://newdivan.org.uk/blog/interview-with-gonca-ozmen/
4. Brodsky, J. (1987). *Less Than Zero.* Penguin.
5. Doherty, N. P. (2022). Eda, or The Herd Writes Back. A Riposte to Joseph Brodsky. Talisman, *A Journal of Contemporary Poetry and Poetics,* 51.
6. Zeka, N. (2003). A Prisoner of Language: The Strange Case of Modern Turkish Poetry. *South Atlantic Quarterly,* 102(2–3).
7. Page, B. (2011, January 26). Orhan Pamuk attacks 'marginalisation' of non-English writers. *The Guardian.* https://www.theguardian.com/books/2011/jan/26/orhan-pamuk-attacks-marginalisation-non-english
8. Parker, T. (2018, May 1). On Turkish Poetry Today: An Interview with Mel Kenne. *The Bosphorus Review of Books.*
9. Firan, C. & Mugur, P.D. with Foster, E. (eds.) (2006). *Born in Utopia: An Anthology of Modern and Contemporary Romanian Poetry.* Talisman House.

Sis Çanları

Fog Bells

Cevat Çapan

Cevat Çapan was born in 1933 in Darıca, Western Turkey. He studied English Literature at the University of Istanbul before moving to Cambridge University to complete his doctoral thesis on Irish theatre. For many years he was known as an indefatigable translator of a huge range of world poets, from Brendan Kennelly to Cavafy, into Turkish. He began to publish his own poetry in 1985 and since then has published some eleven collections as well as countless translations. Arc Publications have published two collections of his work in English translation: *Where Are You, Susie Petschek?* (trans. Michael Hulse and the author, 2001) and *The Sound of Water* (trans. Ruth Christie, 2017). His latest book, *Geceleyin Bir Tren/A Train at Night,* was published in 2023.

Bozkır

Denizi, özledik; denizi
denizin alçalıp yükselişini
külrengi günlerde uçuşan
ak martıları,
büyük sessizlik içinde
geceye doğru
aydınlık, ılık
denizi özledik

The Steppe

It is the sea we've yearned for, the sea,
the rise and fall of the sea
the white seagulls flitting
on ashen days,
in infinite silence
out towards night
we have yearned for the
bright, warm sea.

Walter Benjamin

(1892–1940)

Hayatta çok geç öğrendim
yolumu kaybetmeyi ormanda;
bu yüzden büyülenmiş gibi aşkla,
   dolaştım durdum
sevdiğim şehirlerin sokaklarında.

Düşlerim
karanlık dehlizlerde kaldı,
çocukluk defterlerimin yapraklarında.

Nelerden, nerelerden geçtim
kaybolan zaman ardında.
Kaçmadım, kovalandım, kıstırıldım
   bir sınırda.

Belki de bir kurtuluştu
çıktığım son yolculuk
Tarih'in kılavuzluğunda.

Walter Benjamin

(1892–1940)

Only late in life did I learn
to lose my way in the forest
and so dazzled by love
    I traipsed and traversed
the streets of the cities I revered.

Over dark passages
on the pages of childhood copybooks
my dreams lingered.

What places, what things I saw
in my search for times lost,
and yet I never fled, but was chased,
    cornered at some border post.

Ah but that last journey I set out on,
guided by History herself,
was a sort of liberation, perhaps.

"Uçalım Küçük Asya'nın Ün Salmış Kentlerine"

Dönerken uzaklardan
yıllar sonra yurduma,
Catullus'un Verona'sından
konakladım bir gece.
Arena'da Norma'yı dinledim
o ışıl ışıl kalabalıkta;
kemerli köprülerden geçtim
ay aydınlığında,
düşümde Frigya ovaları,
İznik'in verimli toprakları.

"Let us fly to the far-famed cities of Asia Minor"

Returning home after
years spent in distant lands,
I stopped off for a night
in Catullus' Verona.
In the Arena among that
glittering crowd, I listened to *Norma;*
in the light of the moon
I stepped through arched bridges,
the plains of Phrygia, the fertile lands of Nicea,
luminous in my mind.

Kesin Dönüş

Okuduğum kitapta Polonyalı bir işçi, Paris'ten
düğün için doğduğu kasabaya dönüyor
bir yıldır birlikte yaşadığı sevgilisiyle.
Çocukları da onlara katılacak düğünde.
Giderken boş bıraktığı evinin odalarını
dolaplarını, çekmemecelerini elden geçiriyor
    çalgıcılar gelmeden.
Eski gömlekler,
    yamalı pantolonlar,
        gazete kesikleri ve birden
zarf içindeki fotoğraflar arasında
Rosa Luxemburg'un resmi

Final Return

In the book I was reading, a Polish worker
returns from Paris to the place of his birth to marry
the lover he's been living with for a year.
Their children, too, are to join them at the wedding.
As he leaves, just before the musicians arrive,
he checks through the rooms, the presses and drawers of the house
    he's emptied out.
An old shirt
        patched up trousers
                newspaper cuttings and suddenly
out from among the photographs in an envelope,
a picture of Rosa Luxemburg.

Yaz Bitmeden

Rodos'tan Bodrum'a geçerken
   kayığımla
Dante'yi okudum, demişti Balıkçı,
   ay ışığında.
Paluko teknenin burnunda
suların derinliğini ezberliyordu
mavi gözlerinde batık bir dünya.

     *

Anlattığın o uzak denizlerin
kumsalları da ıslanmış olmalı bu sabah
birden boşalan sağanakla;
belki kayalar bile yumuşamıştır
yağmurlu dalgalarla.

     *

Coğrafyacı Strabon anlatıyor,
çok pınarlı İda'nın eteklerinden
Ege'ye akan ırmaklarının kıyılarındaki
   yeşil ovaları.
Sonra da Zeus'un, kendine şarap sunucusu
yapmak için,
bir kartala dönüşüp pençeleriyle
Kral Tros'un yakışıklı oğlu
   Ganymides'i
nasıl kaçırdığını.

Before the Summer Ends

While crossing from Rhodes to Bodrum
    in my skiff,
the Fisherman said, I read Dante,
    in the moonlight.
Paluko there in the bow
learning the depths of the waters by heart,
a sunken world in his blue eyes.

          *

The strands of those distant seas
you spoke of must be wet this morning,
soaked in the sudden shower;
perhaps even the stones have softened
in the rainy waves.

          *

Strabo the Geographer tells of
the green plains by the banks of the rivers
that flow into the Aegean
    from the many springed slopes of Mt. Ida.
And also of how Zeus turned into an eagle
    and made off in his talons
with Ganymede, the handsome
son of King Tros,
    to have him as his
cup bearer.

The Fisherman of this poem is the novelist, essayist, ethnographer and travel writer Cevat Şakır Kabaağaçlı, better known by his penname, The Fisherman of Halicarnassus. Paluko, Mustafa Esim, was fisherman from Bodrum who became Kabaağaçlı's close friend and confidant.

Gitmediğimiz Adalar Vardır

Dublin'e ilk geldiğimde
uçan seccadeden inermişim gibi karşılamıştı beni
Brendan Behan.
Nazım Hikmet'i sormuştu bir puba girer girmez,
Onu Borstal Hapishanesi'nde okumuş,
"Demir parmaklıklar arasından seyretmiştim,
memleketinizden insan manzaralarını
Şeyh Bedreddin'i de orada tanıdım."

Birlikte Martello Kulesi'ne gittik sonra,
Stephen Dedalus'un hayaletiyle konuştuk
Ağır ağır akan Liffey nehrinin sularını seyrettik.
"Kalender bir Paris'e benzer Dublin" dedi,
"bu kemerli ve kederli köprüleri yüzünden."
O'Connell Caddesinde, Büyük Postane'de
1916 Paskalya Ayaklanması'nda
Kurşuna dizilen asilerin resimlerini gösteriyor
birer birer.

Akşam Abbey Tiyatrosu'nda O'Casey'in
Kırmızı Güller'i.
Oyuncularla tanıştırıyor bizi Eddie Golden
oyun bitince.
"Haftaya Synge'in Acıların Deirdre'si
Başlayacak
izlemeye gelirseniz seviniriz"

Saffet Korkut'un Babayiğit çevirisi geliyor
Aklımıza
Ve Orhan Burian'ın Denize Giden Atlılar.

Denize giden atlara binip Aran Adalarına gidiyoruz
Fırtına çıkmadan

Islands We Have Never Visited

When I first came to Dublin
Brendan Behan
greeted me as if I were stepping off a flying carpet.
Entering a pub, he quizzed me about Nazım Hikmet
Whom he'd read in Hollesley Bay Borstal:
"I peered out through iron bars at
those human landscapes from your country,
and got to know Şeyh Bedreddin too."

Later we went out to the Martello Tower
To converse with the ghost of Stephen Dedalus.
We watched the slowly flowing waters of the Liffey,
"By virtue," he said "of these arched and aching bridges,
Dublin is not unlike some down-at-heel Paris,"
on O'Connell St, in the GPO
he pointed out the pictures of the rebels
executed in the 1916 Rising.

Evening, O'Casey's *Red Roses for Me* at the
Abbey Theatre,
after the performance Eddie Golden introduced us
to the cast,
"Next week Synge's *Deirdre of the Sorrows*
opens,
we'd be delighted if you'd come and see it"

We think of
Saffet Korkut's translation of *The Playboy of the Western World*
And Orhan Burian's *Riders to the Sea.*

On horses to the sea, we ride, making for the Aran Islands
before the storm breaks.

Denizin O Bildik Diliyle

Adlarını gizleyen o kaçak sevgililer,
Nuh'un gemisine yetişmek için
el ele çıktıkları o uzun yolculukta
kara, kapkara bir boşlukta buldular
        kendilerini,
beklenen tufanın gelip gelmediğini
        sormadan.

Sonbaharın sonunda, tam kışa hazırlanırken,
bilmedikleri bir kıyıda, sığınarak
        masalların alacakaranlık mağarasına,
duvarlarda geçmiş zamanın yarı silik,
        ama hala baş döndüren,
                baştan çıkartan resimleri.

Mağaranın dışında bulutlu gök,
        uçurumun boşluğunda
                kartalların sessizliği.
Gene de çözmeye çalışıyorlar şimdi
çivi yazılarının, hiyerogliflerin
ve yarısı silinmiş tabletlerin gizlerini.
Kurtulmanın yollarını arıyorlar
bu umursamaz kalabalığın
        yalnızlığından
ve yeni kıtalar keşfetmek için
öğrenerek denizin o bildik dilini.

In the Familiar Language of the Sea

At one point on the long journey
they'd set out hand-in-hand to find the Ark,
those fugitive, nameless lovers
found themselves in a pitch-black
emptiness
unable to ask if the expected
storm had come or not.

At the end of autumn, while preparing for winter,
on a shore they did not know, they took refuge
in the twilight cave of fable.
On the walls, the faint yet
still dazzling, still tantalising
pictures of the past.

Outside the cave a cloudy sky,
a silence of eagles
in the emptiness of the cliffs.
Yet again, they endeavour to decipher
the secrets of cuneiform, hieroglyph
and half-erased tablets.
As they look too for ways to flee
the solitude of the
uncaring crowd,
and to explore new continents,
while learning the familiar language of the sea.

Torosların Eteklerinde

Demek güneşe de, öbür yıldızlara da yön veren
    sevgiye inanıyorsun sen?
Acı bir gülümsemeyle soruyor bunu emekli albay,
    genç yeğenine.
Hayal gücünün sona erdiği yer mi amcayla yeğenin
    hoşbeş ettikleri bu çardak altı?
Suların, rüzgarın, bulutların, hatta bir söğüdün
    gölgesinin de
duygu dünyamızı etkilediğine inanıyorum ben.
Sizin savaşlarda, belki barışta bile yaşadıklarınız,
    top sesleri, barut kokusu
bütün o yaralı askerler, genç ölüler,
    adresine ulaşamayan mektuplar,
ve kavuşmayan sevgililer? Bütün bunların da
    izi yok mu
        sizin o acı gülümsemenizde?

Atlarına binip yola koyuluyorlar.
İskender de buralardan geçmiş, diyor emekli albay,
Toroslarda, Gülnar'dan Narlıkuyu'ya inerken.

In the Foothills of the Taurus Mountains

In other words, you believe in a love that guides
        the sun and the other stars?
The retired colonel asks his nephew,
        a bitter smile on his face.
Is this bower where uncle and nephew confabulate
the place where imagination ends?
I believe the waters, winds, clouds, even the shade
        of a willow tree
affect the world of our feelings.
And those things you experienced in war, and perhaps in peace too,
the roar of cannons, the smell of gunpowder,
all those wounded soldiers, the young dead,
        letters that never reached their addresses
and lovers destined never again to meet? Is there no
trace of any of these
                in your bitter smile?

They mount their horses and set off.
Alexander once passed through here, the retired colonel says,
as they descend from Gülnar to Narlıkuyu in the Taurus Mountains.

Sonu Gelmeyen Yolculuklar

"Türkçe konuşamamak da oldukça can sıkıcı,"
    diyor Seferis,
yıllar sonra Ankara'da görevli saygın bir Yunan
    diplomatı olarak
çocukluğunu geçirdiği İzmir'in sokaklarını
    dolaşırken.
Daha çok Urla-İskele'deki dayısının evi canlanıyor
    gözünde
ve kulaklarında Rum balıkçıların ezbere okudukları
    Erotokritos destanı.
1950'de bir Temmuz akşamı hava kararırken, kırlardan
    meltemle gelen çiçek kokuları
bitmemiş yolculuklarından birine çıkarıyor
    eski hemşerimizi.
"Nedir ruhlarımızın aradığı, yolculuklara çıkıp," diye
    belki de ilk burada sormuştu kendine.

Kara defneler arasında, koca çınarlar altında, nereye
    demir atacağını bilemeden
kıyıdan kıyıya sürüklenerek, sorarak büyük yangını
    kimin çıkardığını
ve yıkık tapınakları ürkütücü gölgelerinden
    uzaklaşarak
boş, susuz sarnıçlara sesleniyor ve belki
    o da bizim gibi
        hayatın köklerini arıyordu
            bıkmadan.

Never Ending Journeys

"It is somewhat irksome to be unable to speak Turkish,"
        said Seferis,
when years later, as a respected Greek diplomat posted to Ankara,
        he strolled the Izmir streets
        of his childhood.
Yet mostly it was his uncle's house on the quay
        in Urla that he visualised,
his ears ringing with the Epic of Erotokritos the Greek sailors
        all recited by heart.
On a July evening in 1950 as the air grew dark, the scent of flowers
borne on the meadow breezes has our old compatriot embarking
on one of
        his unfinished journeys.
Perhaps it was here that he first asked himself:
"What is it our souls seek as they set out on the road?"

Among the dark laurel trees, under the huge sycamores,
        with no idea where he will drop anchor,
he drifts from shore to shore, wanting to know just who'd started
        that Great Fire
and moving away from the eerie shadows of the
        ruined temples
he calls out to the empty, waterless cistern for perhaps
        just like us
            he is tirelessly
                seeking for the roots of life itself.

Mehmet Taner

Mehmet Taner was born in the province of Nevşehir in Central Anatolia in 1946. He studied drama at the University of Ankara before working as a producer and announcer for TRT, the state television company. He later founded his own insurance company and set up Tan Publishing, a publishing house dedicated solely to poetry. He has published seven books of poetry which were later issued in two volumes by the prestigious Yapı Kredı Publishing House in 1999 and 2002 respectively.

Geniş Soluk

Başkaldırıyorum yalnızlığa
Başkaldırıyorum acıya
Başkaldırıyorum umutsuzluğa

Başkaldırıyorum yoksul düşmüş ruhuma
İçkiye, ağıya ve melale
Çamurun tadına
Sonluluğuna, sonsuzluğuna göğün, yaşamın
Bulanık şiirlere
Küskün yüzüme, bezgin, bıkkın yüzüme
Ey anam, babam, kardaşlarım
Dostlarım, haldaşlarım
Ağaçlarım, ballarım, kuşlarım;
Başkaldırıyorum
Ant içerek
Genç ölülerin taze kanı üzerine;
Ant içerek
Yurduma, konuştuğum dile, ta bana dek ulaşmış
Işığın üzerine;
Ant içerek
Bu ışığı taşımanın
Onuru üzerine!

Hoşça kal sen de ey büyü!
Ey berrak çakıl taşı, ey küçük bulut!
Ey gözlerimin ucunda duran simya!
Hoşça kal, etin ve belleğin parklarında
İç gıcıklayan gece!

Spacious Breath

I am rebelling against loneliness
I am rebelling against pain
I am rebelling against hopelessness

I am rebelling against my impoverished soul
Against drink, poison and boredom
Against the taste of mud
Against the finitude & infinitude of the sky, of life
Against obscure poems
Against my sulky face, my sick & tired face
Oh mother, father, sisters and brothers
My friends, my confidants,
My trees, my honey, my birds;
I am rebelling
By swearing an oath
On the warm blood of the young dead
By swearing an oath
On my homeland, on the language I speak, on the light
That has reached right up to me;
By swearing an oath
On the honour of carrying
This light.

Goodbye to you too, oh magic!
Oh clear pebble, oh tiny cloud!
Oh alchemy, dwelling in the corners of my eyes!
Goodbye to you in the parks of flesh & memory
Unsettling seductive night.

Göç

Gelin daha güzel olsun
Çağrılan mavi aydınlıktan
Derin uçurumlardan, fısıltısından suyun ve incirden
Şevval ayından ve Kudüs'ten
Yangından
Kulübelerden bile daha güzel olsun;
Çırılçıplak kalınca, parmağındaki yüzükten
Nemli dil üstünde duman gibi
Varsayılan bahardan
Uçurumlardan, fısıltısından suyun ve incirden
Gelin daha güzel olsun
Daha civan olsun diye güvey
Feza çağında
Cila tül rimel ruj ve imza kullanıldı

Şevval ayında Kudüs'e sefer kılındı
Ballıbabalar zümrüt ve sair Kafkasya

Exodus

Let the bride be more beautiful
Than the blue light called down
Than the steep cliffs, the whisper of water, than the fig
Than the month of Shawwal, than Jerusalem
Than the fire
More beautiful even than the cabins
Than the ring on her finger stripped bare
Than steam on a damp tongue
From an imaginary springtime
Than the cliffs, the whisper of water, than the fig
Let the bride be more beautiful
So the groom will be more handsome still
In this the space age
Recourse was had to nail polish lace mascara lipstick and signatures

In the month of Shawwal, a campaign was undertaken to Jerusalem
The dead-nettles, emeralds and the other Caucasus

Rübai

Dere ağaçların altından akıp gidiyordu. Yazdı.
Koyu gölgelikte oynayan çocuklar kimbillir hangi sözle büyü-
lenmişti. Kral görkemiyle susmuştum ve susturuyordu ev-
reni bir uçuç böceği yeniden.

İnce perdeyi şişiren yel
Yoksul şarabımı aydınlatıyor

Rubai

River slipping under the trees. Summertime. Who
knows what word bewitched the children playing in the
deep shade. I fell silent in the splendour of a king,
as a ladybird silenced the universe yet again.

The breeze swelling the thin curtains
lights up my poor wine

Böğürtlen

Kokumla yaşıyorum: Dağ, orman kokuyorum ben
Çalı kokuyorum, ıssız bozkırlar kokuyorum, tren kokuyorum.
Patikalarda böğürtlenler korku içinde çekilirler derin yarlardan:
Yılgın serviler kokuyorum, böğürtlen kokuyorum.

Yaşadım bir su gibi, eriyerek;
Köpek havlamaları gibi.
Çınlıyorum da, kimsesiz çocukların uykuya geçmeleri nasıl çınlarsa;
Sonsuz ve mutsuz olanı duyuyorum yalnız.

Blackberry

I live with my smell: I who smell of mountain, of the forest.
I smell of briar, of deserted steppes, I smell of the train.
On the paths, the blackberries retreat in fear of steep slopes,
I smell of daunted cypress trees; I smell of blackberry.

Like frozen water I have lived, always melting;
Like the barking of dogs.
I too ring out, just as abandoned children ring out as they tumble
        into sleep;
All I hear, the unending, the unhappy.

Çin Şiirleri

1

Seninle söyleştiğimiz o bahçede
Oturup şiirlerini yazdım
Eski günlerin

Nasıl yağmur vardı o gün, nasıl elektrik

2

Kapıcı kızları bal topluyor
Bahçede, kırmızı hırkalarıyla
Benim içimde
Bal yok, bal yok

3

"Üç top ışık patladı"
Akşam ile
Üç ağacın üstünde

Biri açık
Öbürü dönük içe
Üçüncü
Kapalı iyice.

Üç top ışık patladı
Üçü de
Parlak birbirinde

Chinese Poems

1.

In the garden where we parleyed
I sat & wrote
Poems of days past

That day, what rain! what electricity!

2.

The janitor's daughters are gathering honey
In the garden, their cardigans all red
But in me
There is no honey, no honey at all.

3.

'Three balls of light burst'
Over evening
& over three trees

One open
The other withdrawn
The third fully
Closed

Three balls of light burst
Each one brighter
than the other

Derviş

Adam ansızın yolumu çeldi. Kolunu uzatıp
Çekti önüme yığdı sabahı.
Şarkılarla koca bir dağ yaptı, atılmış şarkılarla
Sonra bir yumaktan söker gibi
Açtı dağı. Bir yandan açtı, yürüdü bir yandan:
– Bu bir sanrı olsa olsa
Dedi,

Çünkü ben, gözleri olmayan ben
Nereye gittiğimi bilmem ki.

The Dervish

Abruptly blocking my path, the man. Stretched out
His arm, heaped the morning up before me.
Of song he made a mountain of discarded song.
Before splitting open the mountain as if he were
Unwinding a ball of wool, splitting it open as he walked:
– If anything, this is but an illusion,
He said,

For I, I who have no eyes, never know
Just where it is I am going.

Ateş

Bunları ilgiyle dinleyen ey deniz, suskun ana
Seni anladım işte ter içindeyim

Sabaha yetişen avcı!
Çıkar üstünü, as tüfeğini, gel
Tütün torbamı alıver şurdan
Otur ateşin başına, doldur şarabı
Kar bu yıl düştü epey
Kürk bereketli!

Ay doğunca – Ay

Şerefe! Güne inecek misin bu yıl?
Bu ne tutukluk dilinde!
Üzülme kırığın için, kar sar
İki odun daha atıver, rüzgâr kötü:
Rüzgâr iyi ki kötü
Böyle daha sessiz

İstersen bir tütsü yak kendine
Olmazsa daha da konuşuruz

Fire

Oh sea listening intently to all this, oh you silent mother
I have understood you, so here I am, covered in sweat

Hunter, now that you've reached the morning!
Take off your coat, hang up your rifle, come
And take my tobacco pouch from over there
Sit down at the fire and fill your glass with wine
So much snow has fallen this year
That the fur is abundant!

As the moon rises – The moon

Cheers! Will you be heading south this year?
Some cat must have got your tongue!
Don't fret over that break, bind it in snow
Then throw two logs on the fire, the wind's up:
Be grateful, for
It's quieter this way

If you want you can light some incense for yourself
If not then we can just talk some more.

Lale Müldür

Lale Müldür was born in Aydın, Western Turkey in 1956.
She studied Electronics and Economics in the Middle East
Technical University in Ankara before moving to
Manchester where she completed a degree in economics in
1980. She later studied literary sociology at Essex University
and continued her doctoral studies in Belgium before
returning to Turkey in 1986. To date she has published
fifteen collections of poetry, a novel and two books of essays.

yağmur yatağı

barbar bitkiler gibi yerleşiyorsun alana ... sen gelince
bir buğu sarıyor çiçekleri ... üzerimizden yeşil bir
dalga gibi geçen sessizliği görmüyorsun ... asıl barbar
benim oysa yansıtamadığı dillerle kuşatılmış ...
kapıyı hızla çarptığında bir su çizgisi yok oluyor önce
sonra beni kuşatan diller ... duvarlarda beliren
mor lekelere bakıyorum hiçbir şey söylemeden ...

ona ince uzun bir yaprak uzatıyor ve diyorum ki:
... hiç korkma benim dokum cam ...
... *ölmüştüm ... ama işte şimdi yeniden yaşayanım* ...
... bende hiçbir şey yok bir çığlıktan başka ... yosun ...
... denizaltı odaları ... bir yağmur yatağından başka ...

bed of rain

like barbarian plants you settle in the clearing … when you arrive
a mist enshrouds the flowers … and you don't see
silence passing like a green wave over our heads … but the real
    barbarian
is me besieged by languages she cannot reflect …
when suddenly you slam the door, first the waterline dissipates
and then those languages besieging me … without uttering a
single word I stare at the purple stains appearing on the wall

I hold out a long thin branch to him and say:
… don't be afraid my texture's spun from glass …
… once I died … but am again among the living …
… I've nothing but a scream … some seaweed …
… chambers under water … nothing but a bed of rain …

Bachmann'a – J. Brel'e – Istanbul Dostlarına Mektup

Ne çok şey eskidi diyorsun
Benim küçük intiharlarım
Kimseler yoktu Tarot kahvesinde
Birileri teneke çalıyordu dışarda
Artık çıkış kimseyi ilgilendirmediğinde
Yaprakların dilini konuşmak gölgelerin
Yeni bir dünya yok
Yeni bir dil olmadan
Söyleyemediklerim yaralıyor en çok
Aradığım ne varsa bulamıyorum
Kim bana bir iris bıraktı terk ederken beni?

Uzaklarda deniz-kızları ölüyor
Bir kadının görebileceği bütün düşler
Amazonya, yüreğim …

Tekrarlanan bir dil/tekrarlanan bir dünya
Deka-dans-ia
Bir ikonun, bir personanın etrafında döndü her şey
Ne çok kişi bıçaklayıp durdu kendini
Gecelerden bir gece Manresa'da olmak
Mutlak değerlerin çekiminde adım atmak
Mermer yüzlerle
Demode zevklere doğru
Unutmak deka-dansı unutmak

Ama bu gece Manresa yok
Brüksel'e yağmur yağıyor
Ve bütün kentlerde bir ve tek korku var
Ne çok şey eskidi diyorsun
Değişen bir şey yok oysa

A Letter to I. Bachman, J. Brel and friends in Istanbul

How much has grown old you say
My suicides so small
Bu there wasn't a soul in the Tarot café
Just some people beating on tin cans
When the exit is of no interest to anyone
It's best to speak the language of leaves, of shadows
There is no new world
Without a new language
What I cannot say is what wounds the most
I never found a single thing I searched for
But who, while abandoning me, left me an iris?

Far off the mermaids are dying
All the dreams a woman may have
Amazonia, my heart …

A repeated language/a repeated world
Deca-danc-ia
Everything spinning about an ikon, a persona
How many stabbed and stabbed themselves again
Just to be in Manresa on a night among nights,
And to step, with faces of marble,
In the attraction of absolute value
Towards pleasures long out-of-date,
To forget the deca-dance to forget …

But tonight there is no Manresa
It is raining on Brussels
And in each and every city there is but a single fear
You say, how much has grown old
Yet, in truth, nothing has actually changed

Korkunç akşamüstüler hatırlıyorum
Bitimsiz bir iç sıkıntısıyla
Küçük bir odada birlikteydik
Birileri Krilov'du
Birileri Nastasya Filipovna
Birileri ormanda keman çaldı tek başına
Herkes kendi Marienbad'ını yaşadı
Hortlak yaşamların gölgesine doğru
Ölmedi onlar
Başka bir biçimde aynı şeyleri yaşıyorlar

Küçük bir odada birlikteydik
Odalar büyüdükçe birlikte olunamıyor

I remember those awful afternoons
Filed with never-ending tedium
All of us together in a small room
Some were Kirilov
Some Nastasya Filippovna
And others played the violin alone in the forest
While into the shadows of ghostly lives
Everyone lived out their own Marienbad
They have not died, but in another shape
Are undergoing the same things again

All of us together in a small room
Though there is no coming together
                    as the rooms grow bigger …

Bir Yağmur Penceresinden

bir yağmur penceresinden
sizi görüyorum
        Visione

ünikornlar aşk yaralarıyla
        uyuyorlar
siz camları kırılmış
bir serada keman
        çalıyorsunuz

bir yağmur penceresinden
sizi görüyorum
        Visione
kırılgan parmaklarınız
olmayan bir müziği
        çalıyor

bir nehiraltı bitkileri seli
ağustos yok oluyor ince
        uğultularla
suları azalan nehirler
kilitli yüreklere kazıyor
        yatakları

bir sonbahar penceresinden
bir fresk görüyorum
        Visione
yıldızların dökülüşü görüyorum
bir incir ağacı
ağır bir rüzgarla
çarpılmış gibi

From a Window of Rain

from a window of rain
I see you
        Visione

the unicorns asleep with
    their wounds of love
as you play the violin
    in a shattered glasshouse

from a window of rain
I see you
        Visione
your fragile fingers
conjure an unearthly
        music

in a flood of riverine plants
august is destroyed by
      fine screams
rivers in drought
dig their beds onto
    hearts under lock and key

through a window of autumn
I see a fresco
        Visione
I see the spilling of the stars
like a fig tree
struck in a
strong wind

toprak renklerine bakıyorsunuz
atların gelişini görüyorsunuz
          VISIONE
mitlerin ölümünü

ve insanlar hiçbir şeye aldırmıyorlar artık

bir gün bir nehiraltı bitkileri selinde
duracak ve
              "her şey öldü, Visione"
diyeceğim.

you look at the colours of earth
you see the coming of the horses
                    VISIONE
and the death of myth

people care for nothing anymore

one day in a flood of riverine plants
I will stop and
                    say
"everything has passed away, Visione"

Yeryüzünde Kaçak ve Serseri Olacaksın: TCDD

kuzeyde erken kalktığım sabahlar, çiçeklerden
yayılan buğu sanki hala havada asılı olurdu.
sonra güneş yavaşça ısıtmaya başladığında, seralarda
yerleşip kalan türden bir koku/nem ortaya çıkardı.
içerde, yatak odasında, o uyuyor olurdu.
bu türden yalnızlık anları, birliktelik-içinde-yalnızlık
anları, başka türlü söylemek gerekirse, onun-içeride-
uyuduğu-türden yalnızlık anları, benim en hoşuma giden
anlar olurdu. ondan geçici olarak, anılarda olsun
uzaklaşmak, yanlış bir özgürleşme duygusu ile birlikte,
bir nane yaprağının sabahın erken saatlerinde azar azar
çiğnenmesine benzer bir tat getirirdi ...
       izmir ... meltem ... ökaliptus
böyle anı uzaklıklarında kalkış yeri kaçınılmaz
olarak kuzey, varış yerleri ise değişmez bir biçimde
daha önce yaşadığım yerler olurdu.

You Will be a Fugitive, a Vagabond on this Earth: Turkish State Railways

on those mornings in the north when I'd arise early, it was as if
the vapour lifting from the flowers was still there, hanging in the air.
then when the sun began to warm up, the smell/ the dampness
that tends to linger in greenhouses would make itself felt.
inside, in the bedroom, he'd be fast asleep. those moments
of loneliness, those moments of loneliness within togetherness,
or to put it a different way, those moments of loneliness while
he was inside sleeping, were the moments I prized the most.
to be temporarily away from him even if it were just in memories,
would bring, alongside a false sense of liberation,
a taste like slowly chewing a mint leaf in the early morning …
        izmir … the etesian winds … eucalyptus …
in those distances of memory the place of departure was inevitably
the north, while the places of arrival were always
those places where I'd lived before.

Buğu Banyosu

şimdi ismini unuttuğum bir şarkıdan

Kırgızistan'da batık bir vadide
Men seni bela sandım.

Kalbimden uzakta çok uzakta bir kurt öldü.
Şarap kızılı bir lale sızıpdur şimdi oradan farkında mısın?

Geceyarısı batkıları ve al kanlar içinde eşkimden
öle buldum. Yıllar ve yıllar var ki Bizansiyya'nın
tungasında erguvani balıkçıl gibi yaşadım.
Çünk heeç, heç görmedim dosttan vefa. Gözyaşım duştu.

Gözelsiz, vefasız, hakikisiz
Meleksiz, çeçeksiz, heykelsiz
Ben bu yerde yaşamadım.

Sonunda bir gün könlüme bir buğu banyosu yaptım.
Bulanık bir yağmur yağdı. Batkın eşklerden kendimi
kurtarıp başka bir tür Aşk'lara aldım.
Ben bu Aşk'a düşeli kimse yüzüm bakmaz.
Sevmiş bulundum güzelim gayri ne çare.

Ela gözlerim teninizin en derenlerine getti.
Batıl bir evlenme yaşadım. Sevsem de öldürüyorlardı
Sevmesem de. Düşerler onlar da yıkılıp düşer bir gün.
Heeç ağlamadım. Mavi kuzgun buğday başaklarını sıyırdı.
Gözyaşım duştu. Ben bu yerde heç yaşamadım.

Steam Bath

from a song I've forgotten the name of

In a sunken glen in Kyrgyzstan
I took ye for trouble

Far, so far from me heart a wolf died
Ye know, a tulip o' wine red now oozes there?

In the midnight ruins, wrapped in crimson blood
I perished o' love, I, who fer years and years lived
like a purple heron o'er the splendour of Byzantium.
For nooo loyalty did I get from any friend. Me tears did fall.

I could never be living in this place
with ne'er a trace o' beauty, devotion, truth,
with ne'er a trace o' angel, flower, idol.

Then wan day in steam I bathed me heart.
A rain all blurred fell. From loves ruined I saved myself
To dive inta Loves o' another kind.
Since then, there's not wan looks upon me face.
I loved, a stór; sure, wha' else could I do?

Down to the deeps of yer skin me hazel eyes fared.
A void marriage I endured. And they just kept on killing
Whether I loved or whether I did not. But they'll fall too,
One day they'll tumble right down.
I nevvvver wept. Off ears of wheat glanced the blue raven.
My tears did fall. I could never be living in this place.

Aralık'ın Anvers'inde İki Melek Çıkmazında İki Çıkmaz Melekle Karşılaşan Ofelya'nın Şarkısı

anvers'de bir sokak. İki melez
çıkmazı. hangardan bir deniz-
ci iniyor. caz ve orman seviyor.
marko polo, sevgilim.

> öteki melekle bir başka bo-
> yutta karşılaştık ve tanıştık.

dalga uzaklığıyla geliyor.   pla-
nörler gibi. eliptik yalnızlıklarla.
sirokko sirokko sirokko esiyor.

> bulutların hortumların ana-
> forların biçiminden sözettik.

bir midyenin içinde sıkışıp kal-
mış rutubet ve uyku, geceleyin
mi düşünürler gemiciler.   en
çok. karayı.   arzusunun içinde
dönüp duruyordu.   kamarasın-
daki bir denizci gibi.

> dalgaları hortumları   anlat-
> maya çemberler   silindirler
> yetmiyordu. bunun için yeni
> bir geometrinin keşfedilmesi
> gerekti.

The Song of Ophelia Meeting Two Dead Angels at the Dead End of Two Angels in an Antwerp December

a street in antwerp. the dead end of
two angels.   a mariner descending
from the dock. fond of forests an-
d jazz. marco polo, my love.

       the other angel we met   and got
       to know in a different dimension.

with its distance   the wave comes.
like gliders. with elliptical loneliness-
es. the sirocco, the sirocco, the siro-
cco blows.

       we spoke of the shapes of cloud,
       tornadoes and whirlpools.

damp and sleep trapped inside a mu-
ssel. is it at nights that   seafarers
dream. mostly. of the land.   turning
and tossing in   desire. like a sailor
in his cabin.

       circles and cylinders were never
       capable of explaining waves or
       tornadoes. in order for that   to
       be done. a new geometry had to
       be found.

sonra hastalanıyor, hastalanıyor
hastalanıyordu. goblen ofelya ...
bir istiridyenin dantel kanatları
gibi kapanarak. belirsiz bir alan-
da dekonstrüksiyon sever. del-
ta ofelya. bir elinde kasnak diğe-
rinde mandolin ve pena.

lacivert gözlü bir yarı-tanrı ...
mermer bir oyukta gizlenmiş
korkuyor kendinden. Birkaç
kişi uçurumlardan düşüyor.

sevdiği şeyin arkasından değerli
bir anı'ını gönderen ofelya .... ge-
lecek mi o, gelecek mi yeniden?

indigo gözlü tanrı
ne kadar kincisiniz
bir Molotof kokteyliyle
boğazıma kaçan incisiniz ...

seninle parmaklarımız buğudan bie ikona değiyor.
onunla bir boşluğa. o boşluğun formunu alan bir
kuş durmadan durmadan ağlıyor ....
onunla gençliğimi yitirdim gözlerimi ....
o kloroformlu g ö kler ....
büyük yalnızlıklarıyla ....
konuşurlar her zaman kanlarımızın tuzuyla ....

then she grows ill, ill, grew ill. the
tapestried ophelia ... shutting like
the lace wings of an oyster. in some
uncertain place she loves deconstru-
ction. the delta ophelia. embroidery
frame in one hand, mandolin and pl-
ectrum in the other.

>   a demi-god of navy coloured ey-
>   es ... has hidden. afraid of himself
>   in a marble hollow. a handful of
>   people. tumble from the cliffs.

ophelia who sends   a precious moment
in the wake of the thing she loves ... will
he come, will he come once again?

>   and how full of spite you
>   god with eyes of indigo blue
>   with a molotov in your paw
>   you're the pearl stuck in my craw

you and I, our fingers touch an ikon of steam
and with it an emptiness.   the bird which takes
its shape just cries and cries ....
with it I lost my youth, my eyes ....
those chloroform s k ies ....
with their immense solitude ....
speak always with the salt of our blood ....

'He shot you down, bang, bang'

Seni bir gün en yakının ele verirse eğer,
Öğren susmasını ve ağlamamasını.
Bir kavanozun içinde mavi bir gül
Yetiştir her gün daha çok yaşayan.

Bir masalın ağzını kapat ve YAT
GENİŞ ODALARDA.
BİR OKSİJEN ÇADIRINDA.

O'NA KÖTÜ BİR ŞEY OLSUN İSTEDİM.
BANA AŞIK OLSUN İSTEDİM

'He shot you down, bang, bang'

If, one day, the person closest to you
Should betray you, learn to be silent
And not to cry. Grow a blue rose in a jar,
One that will live more and more each day.

Shut the fairytale up and LIE
DOWN IN SPACIOUS ROOMS
IN AN OXYGEN TENT.

I WANTED SOMETHING BAD TO HAPPEN TO HIM
I WANTED HIM TO FALL IN LOVE WITH ME

Çay Kuarteti

Ben seni hiç üzemem
Papatya çayı yapmak isterim sana
Sonra portakal çayı
Füme lapsang souchong çayı
Ama ben seni hiç üzemem
Deliririm yalnızca
Sessizce tek başıma deliririm
Beni Lape'ye koyarlar
Koyu Türk çayı içerim orada
Yalnızca

Tea Quartet

I would never upset you
I just want to make you some camomile
And then some orange tea or
Smoked lapsang souchong
But I would never upset you
I would just go mad
Quietly and on my own
They would put me in La Paix*
Where I would drink strong Turkish tea
Only

*La Paix Hospital, often considered to be the first modern
psychiatric hospital in Turkey.

Mustafa Köz

Mustafa Köz was born in Niğde in Central Turkey in 1959. He studied business administration, journalism and law, and worked as a journalist, his articles and essays have been published in magazines and prominent newspapers. He has served on the boards of many literary magazines and festivals. He has been politically active throughout his writing career and since 2014 has served as the vice-president of the Turkish Writers' Union. To date he has published eighteen collections of poetry as well as children's poetry, textbooks, aphorisms and critical essays.

Kör Demirci

Kimsenin izi kalmamış dükkanımda,
tek kişiyi anımsamıyorum bunca zaman
arada bir geliyorlar adanın köylüleri
heybelerinde kuru tuzdan yıldızlar
paslı at nalları, çocuklarının aşı kağıtları
mahkeme ilamları, gazete kesikleri, dalgınlıkları
denizden uzağız, diyorlar
bakarak bir istiridye kabuğuna
vitrindeki bir kenevir rodasına bazen de,
bir kovanın ipi boşalıyor konuştuklarında,
dövülmüş ahtapot rengini alıyor koşumlar
üzengiler, sıra boncuklar, alışkanlıkları, giysileri,
Birkaç iyi söz yetiyor örsü taşımam için
ateşi tutmam için yalın parmaklarımla
zorluyorlar tahta kapının dikey çanını.

Sessizlik, çekirgeler gibi yer değiştiriyor adada.

The Blind Blacksmith

There's no trace of anyone left in my forge
for an age now, I can't recall a single person
yet from time to time they come, the island villagers
stars of dried salt, rusted horseshoes, their children's
vaccination papers, court orders, newspaper cuttings
and pensiveness in their saddle bags
we are far from the sea they say
looking at the shell of an oyster
or sometimes the hemp in the window,
when they speak the bucket's rope uncoils
and their harnesses, stirrups, beads, habits,
and bridles take on the colour of beaten octopus.
A few kind words are enough for me to carry in the anvil
and for my skinny fingers to stoke the fire
as they pull on the door's upright bell.

Across the island, like crickets, silence changes place.

Helix

Sesler tırmanıyor erik ağacına
öğlenin, ikindinin, akşamın sesleri
bir çocuk ağlaması, bir ilenme
ansızın kapanışı bir dua kitabının,
bir böceğin içten içe kemirmesi
kuru bir kökü,
martıların o bildik yakarışı, öğle sonu.

Küçük çanlar sözlüğü –
Zaman: Kabuklu bir yumuşakça
Lat. Helix
bkz. toprak, çivit mavisi, Ortadoğu'da
                    bir nehir
        bir meyvenin dönmesi düştüğü dala,
        çok uzun sürecek bir sayrılık,
Kuyu kapağı gibi sıkıntılı her şey,
seslerden anlıyorum, otların büyüdüğünü.

Helix

Sounds scale the plum tree,
sounds of noon, of evening, of night
of a child's cry, of cursing
of the sudden closing of a breviary
of an insect gnawing secretly
on a dead root,
of the seagull's familiar entreaty as noon ends.

A lexicon of small bells –
Time: an encrusted mollusc
Lat: Helix
also see: soil, indigo, a river in the
                    Middle East,
          a fruit returning to its branch,
          an abiding illness,
Everything as distressed as the cover of a well,
from these sounds I know the grass now grows.

Yağmur Tohumları

Arada bir değiştirmeli havasını odanın
her yere sinmiş fısıltıları, çığlıkları
ruhlarının kokusuyla dolu kap kacak
nereyi açsak anıları saçılıyor köşe bucağa
durmadan konuşuyorlar eski günlerden
varmış gibi görkemi o acınası zamanın
değiştirmeli iskemlelerin yerlerini
çiçeklerin suyunu yenilmeli arada bir
arada bir temizlemeli buhur kabını.

Ne yapsak oturuyorlar yerlerine yeniden
ne bir karış öne ne bir karış arkaya
ölçüp biçiyorlar kendi boşluklarını
açtığımızdan beri ilk çukuru yağmur tohumlarıyla
kayıplarımızın kemikleriyle ağardığı
　　　　　günden beri gecenin.

Seeds of Rain

The room needs to be aired out once in a while
their whispers and screams have seeped into everything
the pots and pans are full of the smell of their souls
wherever we open, their memories spill out into nooks and crannies
they speak continuously of the old days
as if those pitiful times had some splendour
the chairs need to be moved
and the plants watered once in
a while the incense holder needs to be cleaned.

No matter what we do they sit back in their old places
not one foot forward or one foot back
they measure out the shape of their emptiness
ever since we dug that first pit with the seeds of rain
ever since the day night was whitened by
                    the bones of the missing.

Sürgün

Şafakla çıkmıştık yola
göğün yorganı üstümüzde
gürleyip gelen kızıllığı gösterdi birimiz
ne o parmak kaldı şimdi ne o eski gürleme
büyük savaştan sonra dönmedik yurdumuza
büyük zorluğumuzdan, büyük isteğimizden
biz soruyorlarmış bağlarda, su başlarında
düşündürüyormuş sürgünlüğümüz onları
erinçli değillermiş o günden beri – kaygılı, çalık –
en olmaz zamanlarda düşüyormuşuz akıllarına
saçlarını toplarken, kaldırırken kışlık giysilerini
iğneden geçirirken ipliklerini, yıl sonu balolarında
bir dilenci kederini bir ova gibi sermişken önlerine
bir ölünün ceplerini çekiştirirken sabah rüzgarı
bizi düşünüyorlarmış ama bize ne bu olanlardan
biz sürgünler şafakla çıkmıştık yola, sizler için
topraklarımız için kanlı nalçalarla ezilen.

Exile

We set out on the road at dawn
wrapped in the quilt of the sky
one amongst us pointed at the growling red glow
now neither that finger nor that ancient growl remains
after the great war we never returned home,
in the orchards and on the river banks, it seems they ask of us,
of our great hardship and our great desire
for our exile has made them grow ponderous
and since then, they have known no peace – they're uneasy, awry –
it seems we come to their minds at the worst of times
when they are tying up their hair, putting away their winter clothes,
threading their needles, when a beggar spreads his misery
before them, at a New Year's Ball, or when
the morning wind rifles through the pockets of a dead man
they think of us, it seems, but what to us is this
it was for all of you that we exiles set out on the road at dawn,
for the sake of these lands, crushed under bloody, iron heels.

Kurşuna Dizilme

Duvara sırtını vererek bekledi, zakkumların orada
ötede bir kertenkele uyuyordu
– güneşten soyulmuş bir parça deri –
ilk kurşunu kim atacak bilmiyordu henüz
şu ablak yüzlü savaşçı mı
ya da omuzları yıldızla tıka basa şu genç teğmen
otuzuna yenice değmiş şu çopur korucu
bekliyordu ilk kurşunun dağlamasını düşüncelerini
hazırdı buna benzer şeylere
gözlerini yumdu ve delindi ilk kurşunla öğle güneşi
sonraysa bir ışık seli, bir eski sağanak – avluda.

Facing the Firing Squad

He waits, back to the wall, among the oleanders
just over there, a sleeping lizard
– a scrap of leather peeled from the sun –
he doesn't yet know who will fire the first shot;
that chubby-faced warrior,
or the young lieutenant, his shoulders covered in stars,
or perhaps the pock-marked ranger who's just turned thirty
he waits for the first bullet to cauterize his thoughts,
poised for what is about to happen
he shuts his eyes and the first bullet pierces the noonday sun
then in the courtyard
a flood of light and an ancient downpour.

İkindi Güneşi

Sessizce biriken günler
üst üste yığılan kemikler gibi eski mezarda
bu sessizlikten bir çığlık yapabilir şiirim
ruhum bir yanardağ, uyuyor yurdunda şimdilik
bir söz yetebilir uyandırmaya onu tatlı uykusundan
bir söz, halkımın yakınmalarından bir söz, ilenmelerinden
ö sözdür suskun halkıma verip vereceğim tek armağan
diri bir şiirin ilk dizesi, acılardan ve muştulardan söz eden
bir güneş gibi mırıldana kendi kendine,
bir kış günü, bir ikindi güneşi
tanrının bile unuttuğu sonsuz ve soğuk bir alev.

Mid-afternoon Sun

Silently the days have accrued
like bones heaped up in an old cemetery,
my poetry could weave a scream from this silence
but for now, my spirit is a volcano, slumbering in its own land,
a word would suffice to stir it from its sweet sleep
a word, born of the curses and complaints of my people;
the only present I could and will give to these same silent people:
the first line of a sharp poem that like a sun muttering to itself
speaks of pain, of joy;
a winter's day, a mid-afternoon sun
an abiding, cold flame that even god has forgotten.

Ateşböceği

*"Cemil'im gelir diye kapıyı bacayı açık tuttum, gelir de
duymam diye. Ay geçti, gün geçti, ömrüm geçti,
benim çocuğum gelmedi." —Berfo Kırbayır*

Nasıl yakarsa açık yarayı bozkır ayazı
nasıl kemirirse kuru ahlat kökünü çakmak taşı
nasıl dağılırsa suskunluğu olgun incirin
nasıl sararsa göz kapaklarımızı zorlu uyku
nasıl nehir gibi dolanırsa damarlarım kuru gövdemi
nasıl güllerin, dikenlerin çiyiyle serinlerse tarlalar
nasıl yıldızlarla, yasemin kokusuyla örtülürse yaz göğü.

İşte böyle bekliyorum Cemil'im seni
kederle yalnızlığın sarmaş dolaş gezindiği şu yaşlılıkta,
geceden düzlediğim döşeğin kokunla tıka basa
oğlum, canımın yazı kışı, el gibi durma, kapın açık
yarım kalan kitaplarında altı çizilmiş bir dize gibi
sevinçliyim çıkıp geleceksin diye
iki elimde iki ateşböceği, güneşten ve düşlerden
                    düşlerden ve güneşten

Firefly

"I left the door, the hearth open in case my Cemil would come home and I wouldn't hear him. Months passed, days passed, years passed, my life passed, my child never came home". —Berfo Kırbayır

Just as the steppe frost stings an open wound
just as flint gnaws on the root of a dried wild pear tree
just as the reticence of a ripened fig scatters
just as arduous sleep enfolds our eyelids
just as my veins course like rivers through my dry body
just as the fields are cooled by the dew of roses and thorns
just as the summer sky is shrouded in stars and the scent of jasmine

Is just how I am waiting for you my Cemil
in this old age where sorrow and solitude go hand in hand,
your bed I spread out at night is laden with your smell
my son, the summer and winter of my soul,
don't stand there like a stranger; your door is open
like a line highlighted in your half-read books
I am filled with joy that now you will come
two fireflies in my two hands woven of sun and dreams
                                        of dreams and sun

This poem is taken from the poet's latest collection, Uyandım, Dünya Diye Bir Yerdeyim (I Woke Up in a Place Called the World) dedicated to the Cumartesi Anneleri, Saturday Mothers who have been gathering in various squares in Istanbul on Saturdays to protest the forced disappearance of children/relatives since the 1980 military coup. The speaker here is Berfo Kırbayır whose son Cemil was taken from his home in 1980 by the security forces and never seen again. See also Gonca Özmen's poem, 'The 841ˢᵗ Week'.

Elif Sofya

Elif Sofya was born in Istanbul in 1965. After studying economics at the University of Istanbul she completed a master's degree in Fine Arts at the Istanbul Technical University and worked as a visual artist. To date she has published five collections of poetry in Turkish and in 2020 was awarded the prestigious Attila İlhan Poetry Prize for her 2019 collection *Hayhuy/Hullaballoo*.

Çırak

Bir santurla kırçıl balıkların göğsünden ses aldım
Ses indinde adım büyüdü. Gök yakın.
Kalabalığım açıldı, iklim döndü yüzünü
Fısıltılarla geldiler, geçtiler,
ters yüz bu karanlık.

Dimitri, eğrildi senin çizgilerin
gövdene ağır bir çatlak bıraktım. Al.
Fesat çıraklığım çınlatsın kulağını

Apprentice

I drew sound with a santoor from speckled chests of fish
in tandem with sound grew my name. The sky so close.
My multitude parted, climate turned its face,
in whispers they came, they passed,
this inside out darkness.

Your lines have all bent, Dimitri
to your body I bequeathed a severe cleft. Take it.
Let your ears ring with my sinister apprenticeship

Sincap

Bir kıştan yürüyüp geldin
Gözlerin göğe kapalı kapı kanatları
Seni durduracağım
Dikeceğim kumaşımı gövdene bol

Ben bu hikâyenin sonuna doğruyum
Konunun sıkıştığı sokak arası
ellerimden geçiyor
Çizmelerini çekmiş koşuyor ayrılığın atları

Saklanıyor damarlarımda kızıl saçlı bir sincap
Bu sincabın icabına bakılacak diyorsun
Öfken bir ağaçtan daha hızlı kabuklanıyor
Daha hızlı donuyor
akışını altüst ettiğim sular
Ağzından gözlerine buzdan bir çizgi ilerliyor
Sen kör oluyorsun
Gece mor

Omzumda bir sincapla yolculuğum başlıyor

Squirrel

You came walking out of a winter
Your eyes door hinges shut on the sky
I'll bring you to a halt here
And around your body loosely stitch my cloth

I'm somewhere towards the end of this story
The alleyway where the theme is trapped
Slips through my hands
The horses of separation gallop, their boots pulled up

A red-haired squirrel lurks in my veins
We will have to see about that squirrel you say
Your rage growing a bark faster than any tree
The rivers whose flow I disrupted
Are freezing faster too
A line of ice advances from your mouth to your eyes
You grow blind
The night purple

With a squirrel perched on my shoulder, my journey begins

Domuz

Ona bana bir ağaç vermesi
söylenmişti düşünde
Düşmediği uçurum kalmayan adam
Birkaç gölge toplayarak kaçıyordu

Saat on'du, on yoktu düşünde
Ağaçlar ağzına sığmıyordu
Bitecekken uyanmadan
aramızdan sert seslerin geçişi
Şehir belirmeden
Daha hayvanlar suya eğilirken
Deli misin dedim ona
Değilsin domuzsun
Göğsümde bir yavru yaban domuzu ol, kal

Ağaçların sıkıntısı biter o zaman
Uykunun gürültüsü diner

Pig

In his dream he was told
to give me a tree
gathering a handful of shadow
the man who'd tumbled from every cliff flees

It was ten o'clock, though not in his dream
the trees didn't quite fit in his mouth
before he awoke, just as the passage of the
jarring sounds drew to an end
before the city appeared
as the animals bent down to drink
I asked him are you mad
but no you're not, you're a pig
so stay and be a wild *banbh* in my breast

then the trees will be distressed no more
and the noise of your slumber will quieten down

Devlet İtaat Deneyleri

Yatay çizgiler ekleyerek
Gök gürleyerek korkumuza
Korkunun kokusunu hissederek
İyice çekiliyoruz deliklerimize

Burnunda bir an bir yanılma hissi duyan
Susmayı soylu bulan soyunmayı
Sırtındaki kayadan utanarak bırakan
Şimdi şeklini dağıtacak yağmura yürü
Yürüdükçe çözülür dizdeki bağ
Dildeki sentetik tını
Biz buna bir ezberin parçalanması diyelim
Eklemlerin eklenmesi yerin çekirdeğine
Çekirdeğin silmesi
Tarihte tekerrürde sırıtan sahtekarlığı

Uyumsuzluğa doğru yürü
Sade vatandaş iyi yurttaş
Ve millî meselelerin kompetanı
Bana doğru ilerle
Burası harika diyarı

Experiments in State Obedience

Tracing horizontal lines
Thunder howls at our dread
And smelling this stench of fear
We scurry down into our dens

Your nose suddenly tells you you're mistaken
You, who finds silence noble, who as you undress,
Stops, ashamed of the rock up on your back
Walk now into the rain that will scatter your shape
As you do the shackle around your knees
The artificial tone on your tongue will come undone
Let's call this the shattering of rehearsed truths,
Or the fastening of joints to the earth's core
Or the core's erasure
Of the grinning fraudulence of history's repetition

Walk right into disharmony
Faithful citizen, good burgher,
Expert in all national matters
Walk right over to me
For it's a wonderland here

Kuşların Kuşatması

Denizlerden çekiliyor kuşların anavatanı
Seslerinin titrediği kadar
Titremeden gövdeleri
Birkaç yağmur yukarıda bekliyorlar
Bunlar bana ağır bir yükle
Omurgalarını dağıtan hayvanların
gözlerinden görünüyor.

Mayınlar ve sınırlar ayıklayarak topraktan
Kuşlar kuşatıyor kışlaları
Kuşkusuz kararlı adımları var
Dik yazılara sığmayan çığlıkları
Dışarıya bırakan ağızları

Böyle dümdüz düz ederek ortalığı
Bunu ellerinde bir koz diye bekletmeyerek
Kanatlarına rüzgarları gömüp giderken
biliyorlar
Tarih dene teranede
İnsandan başkaları yok diye

Yok sayılacak kuşların kışlaları kuşatması

The Siege of the Birds

The birds' homeland retreats from the seas
Their voices tremble yet their bodies
Do not
With the rain above, they wait.
Through the eyes of animals,
Spines shattered under heavy loads,
They appear to me

Plucking mines and borders from the soil
The birds besiege the barracks
How decisive their steps now are
Their mouths now letting out screams
That no straight script can shape

And so, never staying their upper hand
They raze everything to the ground
But as they leave, burying their wings in wind,
They know
In that litany called history
There is room for human alone

And this siege of the birds will count for nothing at all.

Alzheimer

Irmaktan geldim çıktım toprağa
Yeryüzü gökyüzünden ayrılmamıştı daha
Uygarlığın kıydığı tarih çok sonraydı hayatı
Çok sonraydı
Ölümün gövdelere dadanması
İlk ağızda gürleyecek bıraktım
Zehirden sözlerimi

Suları kurutan yas
Uzadıkça uzadı
Saçlarıma dokunan seslerin
Çınlaması uzadı
Hayvanlığı ev edindim
Beyin kıvrımlarına yerleşip bir karıncanın
Yaşamayı denedim

Ölümün göğsüne yatmak için
Sürmesek de hayatı
Kafamızın içinde durmaksızın büyüyor
Bellek denen mezarlık
İyi ki demans, neyse ki Alzheimer var.

Alzheimer

From river to soil I emerged
Earth not yet sundered from sea
Much later civilization and its destruction,
Its existence much later
Death's haunting of the body
In roars I placed my words of poison
In the first mouth

The grief that dried the waters
Grew more and more
The voices that touched my hair
Rang out more and more
I made a home in animality
And settling into the curves of an ant's brain
I attempted to live.

Though we don't exist
Merely to lie down in death's heart
This graveyard we call memory
Just grows and grows in our heads so
Be glad dementia exists, be grateful for
Alzheimer and his disease.

Sözlük

Süreç tamamlandı, erimeye başladı
Bildiğim bütün sözleri verdim pazara
Orada kalmadım, aklımı takmadım olacaklara
Kaya kesitleri benden uzakta bekliyor harfleri
Yazıtlara benziyor yüzümün çizgileri
Hareketsiz ve konuşkan bir hava eğrisi
Kavislerin en eğlencelisi dönüyor boşlukta

Etimolojiyi iplemiyor içimdeki yabancı
Konuşuyor komşu dillerin lehçesinde
Büyütüyor akrabalığı
Aklım beni terk etmeyi sevmedi
Ben ne çok istedim oysa ayrılığı
Sessiz kalmayı sese dayanmayı
Söz vermeden anlaşmayı
Dil ölümcül bir yokluğun yapay zekâsı

Dictionary

The process is complete, the thaw has set in
I gave each of my words to the marketplace
I didn't stay there or obsess over what was to happen
Far from me the stone screeds await their letters
The lines on my face are like inscriptions
An immobile but talkative curve in the air
The liveliest of the loops spinning in the emptiness

The stranger within me cares nothing for etymology
And speaks in the dialect of neighbouring tongues
Stressing always our affinity
My mind dislikes the idea of leaving me
But I craved for separation, craved
To be left in silence, to resist sound
To communicate without giving a single word away
Language is but the artificial intelligence of a deadly deficiency.

Birhan Keskin

Birhan Keskin was born in Kırklareli in Turkish Thrace in 1963. She graduated with a degree in Sociology from Istanbul University. In 1984 her poems began to appear in various Turkish periodicals. She has worked as an editor for a number of publishing houses in Istanbul. To date she has published eight collections of poetry in Turkish and *Silk & Love & Flame* (trans. George Messo, 2013, Arc Publications) in English. She has received numerous awards for her poetry, including the prestigious Golden Orange Award.

Yağmur

"now that we're here
how do we get back?"

Çağımın aklında plastik çiçekler açıyor,
gülüyor ve seviniyorlar buna. Oysa yağmur
durmadan yağıyor. Biz odanın ışığını
açana dek yağacakmış.
İki kişilik bir sessizliği buluşturana dek,
bir ritmin içinde, tekrar. Yağacakmış, hayatı
oluşturana dek, tekrar.
Sık sık camdan dışarıya bakıyorsun, odaların dışına
kaçıyorsun, kalmak istediğin bir yer yokmuş,
içindeki ses kaygıyla tanıştırıyormuş seni.
Yağmur: Sessizliğiniz huzursuzluğunuzun sesi
diyormuş size. Yankılanıyormuş yağmur:
Ömrün bir şey anlatıyor sana, ama sen anlamıyorsun!
Yağmur durmadan yağıyormuş:
Hiç bir şet rastgele değildir.
Hiç bir şey rastgele değildir.

Rain

"now that we're here
how do we get back?"

Plastic flowers bloom in the mind of this age,
they laugh and grow pleased at that. Yet the rain
pours down steadily. It seems it will do so until we
turn on the lights in one of the rooms.
Until, in rhythm, it brings this two-handed
silence together, again. It will rain until
it creates life, again.
You stare and stare out the windows and flee
these rooms, there's nowhere you want to be,
the voice within you now introducing you to anxiety
The rain: saying your silence is the voice
of your disquiet. It echoes, the rain:
Your life is telling you something you cannot grasp!
The rain, it seems, continues to pour down:
No single thing is random
No single thing is random at all.

Yolcu

"Şimdi" ve "Burada" olmanın kederine karşı çıkmadım.

Dünyada iki kapılı bir han gibi durmanın
buraya böyle gelmiş olmanın,
geçene yol açmanın, ki içinden rüzgâr geçirmenin
ne büyük güç istediğini anladım. Durmanın ne büyük sabır ...

İçimde yeryüzü konuştukça anlıyorum ki,
bölünmüş bir hatırayım ben
dünyaya dağılan.

Ve şimdi biliyorum neden,
yaş akıyor
atımın sol gözünden.

The Traveller

I didn't object to the sorrow of being "Here" & "Now".

For I realise, what great strength it takes
to stand in this world like an inn with two doors,
to end up here like this, opening the way to all-comers,
just letting the wind whistle through, what great patience it takes
to stand …

I see, as the earth speaks inside me
I'm but a memory splintered &
strewn across the world.

And now too I know why
a tear falls,
from my horse's left eye.

İncir

Ne yaprakları hatırlıyor ne güneşi
Ne de düşmüş dalından
Balı içinde kurumuş bir heves gibi
Duruyor yerinde geçen sonbaharda.

Fig

Neither leaf nor sun does it recall
And yet it has not tumbled from its tree
Its honey within, like dried-up desire
It stands still where it was last Fall.

Ayna

Sen bana elma yerdin eskiden
Ben kocaman bir bardak su sana mutfaktan
İki buğulu ağaç olalım, ben sana
iki serin taş, demiştim, daha o zaman
yan yana, ses veren, yağmur alan.

Sen şimdi oradan,
eteğimdeki taşları çatlatan
sözcükleri getir, yan yana getir.

Mirror

Once to me you'd eat apples
I to you from the kitchen a huge glass of water
Let us be two misty trees, me to you
two cool stones, I said, just then
side by side, speaking, soaking in the rain.

Bring now from there,
those words cracking the stones
in my skirts, bring them side by side

Atlar

Rüzgâr gibiydiler, dünyada biz onlarla rüzgâr gibiydik.
Tuhaf bir boşluk duygusu yaratıyor şimdi
Onların burada olmaması.
Otların sesinin uzak durması da demek bundan ...

...

Rüzgâr gibiydiler, dünyada biz onlarla rüzgâr gibiydik.
Bulutlardan otlardan çayırdan geçer nehre değerdik.
Dağlara göçer dağlardan iner adımızla yaşardık.
Bir şimşek çakımıdır dediydik ömür, bunu onlardan bilirdik.
Yakıcı güneş, mağrur yeldi gençliğimiz
Yaşlımız yüzünde yağmur taşır saçlarını uzatır, ahhhhh
Dı.Dı.Dı.Dı ... dık.

İçimin kederini çeken atlar, yokuşu düz eden atlar.
Kalbimi ısıtan atlar.
Kahverengi bir akşam burada, onlar yoklar.

Horses

They were like wind; in this world we were like wind with them.
Their absence creates
A strange sense of emptiness.
That is why the sound of grass keeps its distance …

…

They were like wind, in this world we were like wind with them.
Passing the clouds, grasses, meadows we touched the river.
Up the mountains, down the mountains we lived by our name.
We said life was a strike of lightning, we got that from them.
The scorching sun, the haughty wind was our youth
Our elders bore the rain on their faces, grew their hair, aaahhhh
we … sa.Id.Id.Id.Id.

Horses that pull their sorrow, horses that flatten the hill.
Horses that warm my heart.
There is a brown coloured evening here, but they are not.

Pu'u 'Ō'ō

Benim kalbim bir hatıraya kalsın
Bu çukur vadiye, kazıdım buraya
Gelsin okusun;
Kimin eli değmişse bir ayrılığa
Tütecek sandığı ocak sönecek
Bir daha hiç görünmeyecek o rüya.

Eski vakitlerdi, küçüktüm, aksaktım
Beni kızımdan kardeşimden etmişlerdi.
Kanatlandığım yol, indiğim vadi
Hiç bitmedi çıktığım göç bir daha.

İçimdeki od'a hiç varamazam
Önüme artık bakamazam men
Yaklaşan şeyi kim örüyor,
bilemezem.

Kırdığım buncacık kabuk
Kırdığım buncacık kabuk

Puʻu ʻŌʻō

Let my heart linger as a memory
Into this hollow valley, I inscribed it
So let them come and read;
If your hand were to brush separation
The hearth you believed blazing will burn out
That dream will appear no more

Back when I was small, when I was lame
They did me out of my daughter, my sister.
Over roads I flew, into valleys I alighted
My exodus knew no end.

I cannoh geh ah the fire within me
Cannoh look straigh ahead no more
So who weaves whah approaches
I dunno.

So tiny the shells I shattered
So tiny the shells I shattered

Sulukule 2008

Yaz! Mango ağaçları meyveye durduğunda
Yaz! Güzel dillere güzel şarkılar indiğinde
Yaz! Küçücük da olsa bir cümle.
De ki; kalbimiz bir primat tedirginliğinde.

Yaz! Bir yere gidiyor dünya, sonra dönmüyor!
Yaz! Ölmeden önce çekmemiz gereken binbir dert.
Yaz! Kısacık bir cümle.
De ki; can eriği gevşiyor.

Yaz! Patlıcanda yangın kokusu var
Yaz! Hayatımız natürmort tadında.
Biz mi, yok artık, şarkı söylemek mi?
De ki; bir bitki çoktur bize, bir siyanobakteri!

Yaz! Atları almışlar, Üsküdar'ı geçmişler!
Yaz! Kara kıtanın bağrında benim evim bir kıştı yavrum.
Şairler bunu böyle açık yazmazlar
Ama sen açık yaz! Nasılsa aldırmazlar.

Yaz! Benim evim bir kıştı, yavrum.

Benim evim bir karıştı!

Sulukule 2008

Write! When the mango trees flush in fruit
Write! When beautiful songs alight on beautiful tongues
Write! A sentence, a short one, will do.
And say: our hearts are locked in a primate's unease.

Write! The world is going somewhere, and will not return!
Write! Of all the pains we must suffer before death
Write! A short, short sentence.
And say: the green plums are growing limp.

Write! There is a smell of burning in the aubergine.
Write! Of our picturesque lives.
What, have us sing? I don't think so ...
And say a plant or even a single cynobacteria is too much for us!

Write! They shut the stable doors long after the horses bolted.
Write! My home was winter in the heart of the dark continent,
my child.
Poets never write it as plainly as that,
But write it plainly, now! They won't pay any heed anyhow.

Write! My home was winter, love!

My home, all upside down!

Gazze

Senden kalkıp başka ellere gidemem
Rüzgâr ve kuytu,
Yağmur ve uykuyduk birbirimize
Aklına geldikçe viran teknelerinde
sev beni.

Gazze'de hava bulutlu on yedi derece,
Nem yüzde 16, rüzgâr saatte 13 kilometre.
Saldırıda ondokuzuncu gün, yirminci gece.
Ölü sayısı binin üstünde, yaralı binlerce.

Şimdi önüme dört çöl fotoğrafı koydum.
Dört mecaz olsun diye serin, kanlı dünyaya
Duygusal konuşmak için şairler var diyor,
Okkadar dallama birileri tv'de Gazze üstüne

Yağmurda karda doluda iki kere sev beni
Altüst edilmiş cümleyim ben senin elinde
Zalimin rişte-i ikbalini bin ah bile bazen
Kesmiyor, gördün işte, delik deşiğim ben.

Naylonlara bezlere sarmışlar, büyümeden ...
Büyümeden allahım bakamam,
bakamam onlara ... onlar mermiden ...
Bu çocuklar korrrrrkunç
Vurulmuş allahım.

İnsan; insan ne ki,
Şeytanın bacağı kırık kalıyor
İnsan derken.

Gaza

I couldn't up and leave you for parts foreign
We were wind and shelter
Rain and sleep to one another,
Whenever it occurs to you on your ruined boats:
love me.

In Gaza the weather is cloudy, seventeen degrees
Humidity 16 percent, wind speed 13 kph,
This is the nineteenth day, the twentieth night of the attack,
The number of dead is over a thousand, the wounded too many
to count.

Now I place four photographs of the desert in front of me,
Let them be four metaphors for this cool, bloody world.
For sentimental talk we have poets or so they were saying,
Those fools on the TV, prattling on about Gaza.

Love me twice in the rain, in the snow, in the hail
In your hands I am a sentence turned on its head,
Sometimes not even a thousand sighs can cut the thread
Of the tyrant's desires, and so now you see me in tatters.

They wrapped them up in plastic, in rags before they could grow
Before they could grow, god I cannot look
I cannot look at them … by bullets they …
God but these children have been riddled
Something fierce.

Human: so, what is the human?
The devil hobbles on a broken leg
When we speak of the human.

Gökçenur Ç.

Gökçenur Ç. was born in Istanbul in 1971 and spent his childhood in a number of cities across Anatolia. He has published six volumes of poetry in Turkish and has also been deeply involved in translation both into and out of Turkish; he was on the editorial board of Ç.N. (Translator's Note), a magazine dedicated to poetry in translation. To date he has published several books of poetry in Turkish translation; among those he has translated are such names as Ocean Vuong, Ursula K. Le Guin and Wallace Stevens. A selection of his poetry in English translation, under the title *The Encyclopaedia of Forgotten Things,* was published by Paperwall Publishing in India in 2021.

Çıplaklığın: Şiirde Örtük Anlam

Kimmiş her gece uyanıp
Hiç Anlatılmayacak Düşler Defteri'ne yeni bir başlık atan

Sola küçük bir adımla sıyrılıyorsun
rüzgârda bir mimoza dalı gibi sallanan
omuzlarından bileklerine
düşürdüğün sabahlığından

Sabahlığın: kireçli bir kuyu bileziği
az önce durduğun yerde ışıyan
çıplaklığın: şiirde örtük anlam

Kimmiş her sabah uyanıp
Hiç Gonderilmeyecek Mektuplar Defteri'ne yeni bir tarih atan

Şurda öpmüştüm seni, Şubattı,
sirki söküyordu yevmiyeli işçiler
mandalina kabukları atmıştık yeşil denize
bir muşmula ağacı gibi
buruşuk ve ekşiydi akşam

Akşam: uzaklaşan bir karavanın renkleri, tökezleyen at,
fırtınada şeker kamışları; ışıyor uzun otlar arasında
fırlatılmış yüzük taşı, yaşam: bozulmuş bir nişan,
bir armağan, al onu, al tak parmağına

Peki ama kimmiş,
taşlara sıkışıp kalan bir çadır çivisiymiş

Your Nakedness: The Implicit Meaning in Poetry

Who is it that wakes every night
and adds a new title to *The Notebook of Dreams That Will Never
   be Told*

With a shimmy to the left you step out
of the nightdress you dropped from
your shoulders down to your ankles
shaking like a mimosa branch in the wind

Your nightdress: a chalk-covered wellhead
shining where you were standing,
your nakedness: the implicit meaning in poetry

Who is it that wakes every morning
and adds a new date to *The Notebook of Letters That Will Never be Sent*

I kissed you just here, it was February
casual workers were taking the circus down
we threw mandarin peels into the green sea
the evening as puckered and sour
as a medlar tree

Evening: the colours of a receding caravan, a stumbling horse,
sugar beet in a storm; it shines like the stone of a ring cast
into the long grasses, life: an engagement broken off,
a gift, go on, take it, and put it on your finger

But who then was
This tent peg stuck between the stones?

Yatağından Kalkmayan'ın Seyahatnamesi'ne Övgü

I.

Şiirlerim halka
halka yayılırken
gölün yüzünde

diye anlatıyor Ahmet Çelebi
Yatağından Kalkmayanın Seyahatnamesi'nde

ben bir taş gibi
dibe gömülüyordum.

*(kör bir gezgin
şemsiye tamircisinin
suyun sesini duymak için
geçerken yerden alıp attığı)*

II.

Dünya eyersiz bir at.
Bir yandan düşmemeye çalışırken,
bir yandan kulağına
sen gerçek olamazsın
diye fısıldıyoruz.

In Praise of the 'Travels of the Traveller who Never Gets Out of Bed'

I.

While my poems
rippled in circles
on the lake surface

explains Ahmet Çelebi
in his *Travels of the Traveller who Never Gets Out of Bed*

I sank into the depths
like a stone

(which the blind travelling
umbrella repairman
took up to hear the sound of water
as he passed by, then cast away)

II.

The world is a saddleless horse.
On one hand we try not to fall off
while on the other
we whisper "you couldn't be real"
into its ear.

İskorpit Çorbası

Suların sultasında bir rasathane bu ada
dedi adam

denize ısırganotu der buralılar
dedi kadın

(toprağın sırtına saplanmış bir yaba
gibi duruyordu kasımpatı tarlasında kış,
adlarına kitlenmişti anlamlar;
kadın bir pars zambağı, adam yanan iskele
ve deniz karakalem bir tanrı eskizi çiziyordu
yağmurun kumlara batmış sessizliğine)

balık çorbası gibi içelim aşkı

dolaşırken denizin sokaklarında rüzgâr

Scorpion Fish Soup

"The island is a lookout in the tides of tyranny"
said the man

"Round here they call the sea the stinging nettle"
said the woman

(winter stood in a field of chrysanthemums
like a pitchfork lodged in the earth's back,
all meanings are imprisoned in their own names;
the woman a tiger-lily, the man a jetty aflame
and the sea sketching a god's portrait in pencil
onto the silence of the rains buried in the sands)

let us drink love like soup

as the wind saunters over the streets of the sea

Artık Alışmalısın Sevişirken Kargaların Gülüşerek Kıçına Bakmasına

1 – Denizin kıyısına vardım; gördüm ülkem sonludur
2 – Çok ayrılık, çok kavuşma, ateşten lâle soğanları taşıyorsun koynunda,
3 – Yazdıkların okunacak, adın unutulmayacak sen unutmaya çalışırken her şeyin adını.
4 – Dedi falcı, dedim herkes görür geleceği ama çok geç olmadan değil.
5 – Bir nehir kaç ağaç boyu kala anlar döküleceğini denize.
6 – Adımı sorma, gelirken başkasının adını inlersem alınma,
7 – *Artık alışmalısın sevişirken kargaların gülüşerek kıçına bakmasına*

Now you better get used to the crows looking and laughing at your arse as you make love

1 – I reached the sea shore; I saw my land was finite.

2 – So many partings, so many reunions, you carry tulip bulbs of fire in your breast.

3 – Your writings will be read; your name will not be forgotten even as you try to forget the name of everything.

4 – Said the fortune teller, I said everyone can see the future but not before it is too late.

5 – How many trees before the shore does a river knows it will spill into the sea?

6 – Do not ask my name, if I groan out the name of another while coming, do not be offended,

7 – *Now you better get used to the crows looking and laughing at your arse as you make love*

Düşünde "Sana Shakespeare'in Belleğini Satacağım" Diyen Sese İnandı

1 – Tek görebildiği renkti sarı, her zaman sarı kravatlar taktı.

2 – Düşünde "Sana Shakespeare'in belleğini satacağım," diyen sese inandı.

3 – Njal Sagaları, Kipling, Heine'nin şiirleri sevdikleri; Stendhal, Zweig, Maupassant, Lovecraft sevmedikleri ...

4 – Dil, bilgeliği sadece taklit edebilir diye yazdırdı asistanına bir keresinde.

5 – Bir dersinde İskenderiye Kütüphanesi yangınından söz ederken, sözcükler sonludur dedi. Biçemler de. Bunun için bir kitap yok olursa, bir gün başka biri onu yeniden yazacaktır.

6 – Bu kadar ölümsüzlük de herkese yetmeli.

7 – *Baston, bozuk paralar, anahtarlık [...] hiç bilmeyecekler gittiğimizi*

He believed the voice that in his dream said, "I will sell you Shakespeare's memory"

1 – The only colour he could see was yellow, he always wore yellow ties.

2 – He believed the voice that in his dream said, "I will sell you Shakespeare's memory".

3 – Among the things he liked The Saga of Njal, Kipling, and the poems of Heine; among those he did not: Stendhal, Zweig, Maupassant, and Lovecraft.

4 – Language can only imitate wisdom he had his assistant once write.

5 – When speaking in a lesson of the fire in the Library of Alexandria, he said words are finite. Literary styles too.
And so if one book should perish, someone else will write it again some day.

6 – That much immortality will have to suffice for everyone.

7 – *Walking sticks, small change, key rings (...) they will never know we've left ...*

Kargalar Konuyor Paslı Olta Kutusuna

Karayel –
kargalar konuyor paslı
olta kutusuna

1 – Om! Şu doludur.
2 – Söze bir inek kadar saygı duymak gerekir.
3 – Nefes onu düzen boğadır, akıl onun danası.
4 – Ey amaç, hatırla! İşleri hatırla!

Masa örtüsünden susam tanelerini toplar gibi parmağının ucuyla
dokunmuştun bileğimdeki bene, saat başı gömleğimi sıyırıp
bakıyorum yerinde duruyor mu diye.

Crows Perching on a Rusty Fishing Tackle Box

The northwest wind –
crows perching on a rusty
fishing tackle box

1 – Om! This is full.
2 – One must esteem the word as much as the cow.
3 – Breath is the bull who copulates with her, the mind her calf.
4 – Oh intention, remember, remember all you have done!

As if it were gathering up sesame seeds from the tablecloth
your fingertip glanced off the mole on my wrist, I roll up my
sleeve on the hour to check if it's still there.

İşte Bu Açıklayabilir Bana Neden Yere Çakılmış Bir Serçe Yavrusu Gibi Baktığını

İki yağmuruz biz
bu güz günü aynı
denize yağan

1 – Bu dünyadan göçen herkes aya gider.
2 – Ay ona yanıt verenleri salar. Yanıt vermeyenleri yağmur
olarak dünyaya geri gönderir.
3 – O, ona sorar: "Ben kimim?" O, "Sen gerçeksin." demelidir.
O, ona sorar "Gerçek ne demek?" O "duyulardan ve yaşam
soluğundan başka herşey gerçektir." demelidir. "Ben, senim.
Sen dünyasın. Sen bu dünyasın." O, onu salıverir.
4 – Ben de yirminci veya on üçüncü ayda doğan babamın
sayesinde yirminci veya on üçüncü ayda doğdum. Böylece
tanrıları bilmem ya da bilmemem gerekiyordu.

*Sonradan öğrendim ki ilk sevişmede tutuşurmuş meleklerin
kanatları, işte bu açıklayabilir dedim o günden beri bana neden
yere çakılmış bir serçe yavrusu gibi baktığını.*

This Might Explain Why You've Been Staring at Me Like a Sparrow Chick Tumbled to the Ground

We are two rains
Falling this autumn day
Onto the same sea

1 – Whoever departs from this world heads for the moon
2 – The moon frees whomever answers her questions. Those
who cannot she sends back to the world as rain
3 – She asks him: "Who am I?" To which he should answer,
"you are reality". She asks him: "What is reality?" To which
he should reply, "everything save the senses and the breath
of life is reality. I am you. You are the world. You are this
world." She, sets him free.
4 – Because of my father, who was born on the twentieth or
thirteenth month, I was born on the twentieth or
thirteenth month. Thus, I was obliged to know or not
know the gods.

I later learnt that angels' wings take flame the first time
they make love, this explains, I said, why ever since that day
you've been staring at me like a sparrow chick tumbled to the
ground.

Neyiydik Birbirimizin?

Günü geldi galiba güzden özür dilemenin
Gözlerimiz kapalı dalgaları dinlerdik
Denizi mi, evi mi neyiydik birbirimizin?
Günü geldi galiba güzden özür dilemenin

Gözlerimiz kapalı dalgaları dinlerdik
Yıldızları gagalayan o kırmızı kuşlar
Ne anlatmak isterdi de biz anlamazdık
Gözlerimiz kapalı dalgaları dinlerdik

Denizi mi, evi mi neyiydik birbirimizin?
Gençlik işte, unutmayız sandık yağmuru
Gömdüğümüz yeri, sandık unutmayız,
Gecesi mi, gizi mi, neyiydik birbirimizin?

İlk aşklar – dipsiz denizlere atılmış taşlar
Günü geldi galiba sizden özür dilemenin

What Were We to Each Other

Seems the day's come to beg autumn's forgiveness
We'd listen to the waves, eyes tightly shut
What were we to each other, house or sea?
Seems the day's come to beg autumn's forgiveness

We'd listen to the waves, eyes tightly shut
What did those red birds pecking at the stars
Wish to tell us that we couldn't make out
We'd listen to the waves, eyes tightly shut

What were we to each other, house or sea?
So young we thought we'd never forget the rain
Never forget, we thought, where we buried it
So what were we to each other, night or secret?

First loves – stones cast into a fathomless sea
Seems the day's come to beg your forgiveness

Gonca Özmen

Gonca Özmen was born in Burdur, Southern Turkey, 1982. She studied English Language/Literature at the University of Istanbul, and was awarded a PhD in 2016 for a thesis on Ekphrastic Poetry. She has published three books of poetry, many essays and critical articles to date. A selection of her poetry entitled *The Sea Within* was published in George Messo's translation by Shearsman in 2011. Elif Verlag published her second book *Belki Sessiz* in Monika Carbe's German in 2017. She has won many awards for her poetry, including the prestigious Yunus Nadi Prize which was awarded to her third collection, *Bile İsteye/Knowingly, Willingly* in December 2020. She is also an active translator and has translated a great range of poets as well a number of children's books into Turkish. She is currently working on a translation of Sylvia Plath's *Collected Poems* into Turkish.

Ağzındı

Ağzındı
Çıplak duvar, mahrem kapı

Ağzındı
Doğmamış dizeler getirip bıraktı

İklim değiştirdi otlar kendiliğinden
Gördüm ağzın yaprak kırgınlığı

Ağzındı
Yıkılan ceviz ağaçları gibi

Tüm sesleri toplayıp gitti

Ağzındı
Sokak çocuğum, eksik göğüm

Ağzındı
Ve çocuktuk hâlâ sevişirken
(iki oyun arası)

It Was Your Mouth

It was your mouth
Bare wall, secret gate

It was your mouth
That bore unborn lines of verse

Instinctively the grasses put on another climate
I saw your mouth's leafy bitterness

It was your mouth
Like felled walnut trees

That gathered up all the sounds and fled

It was your mouth
My street urchin, my missing sky

It was your mouth
And we still children when making love
(between two games)

Melez

Dante okudum bir erkeği soydum beyaz
Usul uslu uzandım borçlarımı saydım
Yitiğim çok, avuntum bol, günahım güzel
Bakın işte çalı çırpı kaldım

Kuşları sordum ormana daldım beyaz
Üstümü başımı alıp çıkardım
Ne de güzel durdum omzunla akşam arasında
Uzun uzak hatmilere baktım

Dante okudum bir askeri öptüm beyaz
Bütün kasaba uykuda gibi bir zaman
Attığın taşın yankısıydım geri döndüm
Dünya bazen, bazen dünya sadece kan

Oturdum sonra susacak bir ağız buldum
Karışmıştık kimsesiz ve beyaz
Kitabım, kutsalım, melez çocuğum
Ben sendendir kötü koktum

Dante okudum bir devleti vurdum siyah

Hybrid

I read Dante, stripped a man white
Meekly I lay down to tally up my debts
My losses many, comforts plenty, my sins so sweet
See how I've turned to briar and bramble

I asked after the birds, dived into the woods
I undressed myself there and fled
How lovely to stand between your shoulder and evening
I peered long at the mallow flowers far off

I read Dante, kissed a soldier white
Like a time when the whole town was asleep
I returned the echo of the stone you cast
The world is sometimes, sometimes the world is mere blood

I sat and found a mouth to fall silent in
We grew entangled then forlorn and white
My book, my scripture, my hybrid child
It's because of you that I reek

I read Dante, shot down the state black

Kuzum

Said devrim diyor. Benim saçlarım topuz.
Said'le ikimizin ağzı aralık. Sesler alıp sesler veriyoruz.
Sümeyra'ya inanıyoruz. Benim saçlarım topuz.

Yanına kıvrılana git demiyor hiç Said. Kuzum diyor.
Yanıma kıvrılana git demiyorum hiç ben.
Jar û Evin. Jar û Evin.

Yunacak su bulsam su bulsam ben yunacak
Saçlarım böyle topuz. Böyle fersiz. Böyle derli toplu.

Biri kurban olayım deyince korkuyorum ben.
Ben korktukça gövdemin çanları bir başka çalıyor.
Ben korktukça tekeler çiftleşiyor bağır çağır.

Kuzum diyorlar bana – kuzum diyorum onlara.

Said katliam diyor. Benim saçlarım topuz.
Said'le ikimizin ağzı karanlık. Ölümler alıp ölümler veriyoruz.
Süleyman'a inanıyoruz. Benim saçlarım topuz.

Kanacak yar bulsam yâr bulsam ben kanacak
Saçlarım böyle topuz. Böyle dilsiz. Böyle ferfecir.

My Lamb

Said says revolution. My hair tied up in a bun.
Said and I, our mouths ajar. In sounds we breathe out sounds
    we breathe.
Trusting all the while in Sümeyra. My hair tied up in a bun.

To whoever's curled up beside him Said never says go 'way.
    My lamb he says.
To whosever's curled up beside me I never say go 'way.
Jar û Evin. Jar û Evin.

Could I but find cleansing water I'd cleanse myself.
My hair tied up this way. Lustreless – like so. Tidy – like so.

I am afraid when anyone says for you, I could die.
The more I grow afraid the more the bells of my body toll.
The more I grow afraid more rowdily the goats mate.

My lamb they say to me – my lamb I say to them.

Said says slaughter. My hair tied up in a bun.
Said and I, our mouths dark. In the dead we breathe out the dead
    we breathe.
Trusting all the while in Süleyman. My hair tied up in a bun.

Could I but find a believing lover I'd believe myself.
My hair tied up this way. Muted – like so. Dawn – like so.

Jar û Evin: Kurdish, love and poison

Göle Yas

Eski bir gölsem kuytuda
Azaldıysam gün be gün
Uzundur dindiysem
Bitiverecekmiş olduysam

Kök ver kök ver kök ver

Sonsuz bir girdapta uyuyorsam
Örtük, sözün ve tenin altında
Ağırsam kalbime
Susakaldıysam
Dipte – derinde

Ses ver ses ver ses ver

Düğüm düğümsem
Yorulmuşsam yankıma bakmaktan
Gidilmeyene gidiyorsam aklımdan
Kuşlar başlayacaksa az sonra

Dal ver dal ver dal ver

Uzun bir zılgıtsam
Beklemiş, gecikmiş, kekre
Ölüyorsam
Sicim sicim akmaktan

Can ver can ver can ver

Karaysam şimdi kapkara kederden
Kurum tutmuş
Tükenmeye durmuşsam
Bitkin düşmüşsem beklemekten

El ver el ver el ver

Lament for the Lake

If I'm an old lake hidden away
Waning each and every day
And if I've ebbed for an age
Come to the very end

Roots, roots oh give me roots

If I sleep in a ceaseless whirlpool
Buried under skin and word
And if I'm a burden to my own heart
Fallen silent down in the depths

A voice, a voice oh give me a voice

If I'm tangled up in knots
Weary of staring at my echo
And if in my mind I go where I cannot
As the birds are about to take wing

A branch, a branch, oh give me a branch

If I'm a long-keening howl
Expected, belated and bitter
And if I'm withered away
Trickling now in threads

Breath, breath oh give me breath.

If I'm darkened with the darkest
Layer of soot
And if I've run dry
Drained from all this waiting

A hand, a hand oh give me a hand

Tante Rosa ve Ölümcül Şeyler

"Eski bir günü kurcalamak
ölü bir kuşu yolmak kadar kolaydı"
—Oktay Rifat

Hem neden anlatmalı
        üzerime bir tüy düştüğünü

Neyi nereye koymalı
        sesimin çatlağını

Ağzı ölünün
Ölünün ağzı
Karıştı toprağa

Daha dün buradaydı. Duruyorlardı işte yan yana.
Roma'dan almıştım. Kayıyordu tabanları. Yanımda o vardı.
Onun hep yanımda hep oluşu hep beni hep çok hep boğardı!
Değildik ki biz bir çift ayakkabı – kayardı.

Ayakları ölünün
Ölünün ayakları
Karıştı toza

Demincek buradaydı. Ağzımda acı badem tadı.
At arabalarının dünyadan kalktığı bir zamandı.
Hem bir at olarak neydi ki rüyası. Alnı kırçıldı.
O hep her şeye hep dörtnala hep kızardı.

Kolları ölünün
Ölünün kolları
Karıştı ayaza

Tante Rosa and the Deadly Things

"As easy to pluck a dead bird
as it was to rake over a bygone day"
—Oktay Rifat

Why should the feather
　　　　　that fell on me be told

Where should the crack
　　　　　in my voice be put

The mouth of the dead
The dead mouth
Mingled in clay

Only yesterday they were here. Side by side, just standing there.
In Rome I bought them. The soles all slippery. He was with me.
Always having him always with me always suffocated me!
We were not even a pair of shoes – all slippery.

The feet of the dead
The dead feet
Mingled in dust

They were just here. In my mouth a taste of bitter almond.
It was a time when the horse and cart vanished from the world.
What then was this dream of a horse? Its forehead all grey.
Always galloping always at everything always in anger.

The arms of the dead
The dead arms
Mingled in frost

Hem nasıl anlatmalı
    ölü bir kuşun kanadını

Mezarını kazacağım sözcüğü
    nereden bulmalı

Bir şiirinde Neruda ayakkabı giydirmişti zamana.
Rosa, ah Rosa, ne oldu söyle göğsünde koşturan o ata.
Öyle çok severdi ki soluk soluğa – dönüyor dünya son hızla.
Çağırma artık çağırma. Yer açılsın aklında.

Sesi ölünün
Ölünün sesi
Karıştı uykuya

Mayının da toprağa gömüldüğünü yeni öğrendi Rosa.
Kaçtı bir kemancıyla. Ah Rosa, balkabağından olur mu hiç
araba.
Bir çalılığın içinden geçmek gibi. Siste kuş sanki.
Onun artık hiç olmadığı yanımda hep bir kar tadı.

Demindi. Gözümü açıp kapattım gibiydi.
Ayakkabısının tekini kaybedeni kim ne etsindi.
Silahsız avlıyoruz artık birbirimizi. Delik deşik bir ağ.
Onun elleri hep ince hep uzaklardan hep ısrarla hep gelirdi.

Rosa bazen küser bazen kır çiçeklerine bazen susmaya giderdi.

Bir ölüden daha ölü.

How can the wings of
         the dead bird be told

Where to find the word
         whose grave I'll dig

In one of his poems Neruda puts shoes on time.
Rosa, ah Rosa, what became of that horse galloping on your chest.
How breathlessly he loved – the world spinning at full tilt.
Don't call them back, don't let them crowd your mind.

The voice of the dead
The dead voice
Mingled in silence

Rosa has learnt that mines too are buried in the ground.
She eloped with a fiddler. Ah Rosa, could a carriage ever be of
     pumpkin.
As if breezing through a bush. That bird in the mist.
At my side where he no longer is, a taste always of snow.

It was just then. As if I'd opened and shut my eyes.
What to do with someone who's lost one of their shoes.
Now we hunt each other, unarmed. A tattered and torn net.
His slender hands always insistent always coming always from
     far away.

Rosa grows cross sometimes goes to the wildflowers sometimes
to be silent sometimes.

More dead than the dead.

Tante Rosa: character in a book of thematically linked
short stories by Sevgi Soysal.

Siste Ölüler ve Katırlar

Beyaz tişörte neşeyle sıçrayan domates
Kurudu.

Korkumu gömdüm. Kaskatı. Gülyazı'ya.
Artık burda eşelenmek istiyorum.
Bu darı ambarında. Buraya dünya diyorlar.
Yaralı bir katırın sesi dolanıyor buralarda.

İnce bir sis gibi geçip gitmek istiyor insan.
Tekrarsız.

Nerdesin şimdi Rosa?
Bu cesetleri kim koydu aramıza? Katırlarla.

Ülkesini yitirmişin biri. Tetikte.
Buraya dünya diyorlar. Bu tabuttan evlere.
Denizi görmüş müydük başka yerde?

Annem kalbini söküyor yan odada.
Birbirine dolanmış iki ip. Boşluk gibi bir şey.
Ölemeyen biri çırpınıp duruyor yan odada.

Buraya dünya diyorlar. Can havliyle.
Atıklarımızı ayrıştırdığımız bu yere.

Seğiren bir an. Sıçrayan bir geyiğe benzer.

Seni gömdüm. Kemiklerinle. Ağzın yerinde mi?
Siste Rosa. Siste ölüler ve katırlar.

"Ölmek yeni bir şey değil dünyada" diyor Yesenin.

The Dead and the Mules in the Fog

The tomato that gleefully splattered the white T-shirt
Has dried.

My fear I buried. Rigid. Into Gülyazı.
I want to scratch about here.
In this granary. They call this place the world.
Where the sound of a wounded mule shuffles around.

You want to pass by like a thin fog.
Just once.

Where are you now, Rosa?
Who put these corpses among us? On mules.

Somebody who lost their homeland. Now wary.
They call this place the world. These coffin-like houses.
Had we seen the sea some other place?

My mother's unravelling her heart in the next room.
Two ropes entwined. Something like emptiness.
In the next room there's a person who can't die thrashing about.

They call this place the world. Desperately.
This place where we sort our waste.

A twitching moment. Like a deer leaping.
I buried you. Bones and all. Your mouth's still there?
In the fog, Rosa. The dead and the mules in the fog.

"Dying is nothing new in this world" says Yesenin.

Dünya sisli bir yer Rosa. Dünya ölünen bir yer.
Ansızın bir yabanıl kuş konuncaya kadar üstüne.

Bir gün ben de giderim Rosa. Giderim siste.
Upuzun, dümdüz, üç kere iyi bilinmeye.

This world is so foggy, Rosa. This world is a place to die.
Until suddenly a wild bird perches on you.

One day I too will go, Rosa. Pass by in the fog.
Stretched out, flat, three times to be known to be good.

*This poem refers to the Roboski Massacre of December 28, 2011,
when the Turkish Air Force bombed a group of Kurdish civilians
near Gülyazı on the Turkey-Iraq border, killing 34.*

841. Hafta

Değil öyle değil geç değil değil burası bize yurt değil
Değil boşluğa ayarlı sarkaç desem değil değil o değil
Yan yana bir sürü çam kozalağı da değil hiçbiri değil
Değil sütümüz beyaz değil değil sütümüz sizin değil
Onun gölgesi değil değil güneş bile eski güneş değil
Değil değil dahası değil fazlası değil değil değil değil

— *Sütte Ne Çok Kan*!

Kaç yüzyıl yaşlandık burdan ötesi işkenceli ayak sesi
Zorla kaybetme yöntemi, Madres de Plaza de Mayo
Guatemala, El Salvador burdan ötesi Filipinler, Cezayir
Burdan ötesi yok mezar var cunta – yok utanç var polis
Burdan ötesi Filistin askısı – Bandista, Bandista, Bandista!
Burdan ötesi "iyi dayandın it!" Suç, uydurulan bir şey nasılsa.

— *Ülke geneli için sis uyarısı*!

Kanat sesi şimdi var. Şuracığımızda. Kanat sesi şimdi yok.
Kasım Alpsoy şimdi var. Kasım Alpsoy şimdi yok.
Cemil Kırbayır şimdi var. Cemil Kırbayır şimdi yok.
Agit Akipa şimdi var. Agit Akipa şimdi yok. Yok. Yok.
Yoklamada eksik ne çok – bir midye birden kapanmış gibi.
Silmişler sanki yazılanları – yasssssaaaak insanları.

— *Aparición con vida de los Detenidos – Desaparecidos*!

Unutmadık hiç unutmadık memeyi buldukları ânı. AN ki NE –
Düşürülen dava dilekçesi, tozlu dosyalar, devrik süt güğümleri
Girilen ama asla çıkılamayan binalar, maskeli saray oyunları
Bir yeşil ormanda dallı budaklı, bir ıssız ormanda kollu bacaklı

The 841ˢᵗ Week

No, no, it's not like that, it's not too late, this place is no home
    to us not
No, not a pendulum set to the void, no, it's not that not
So many pine cones side by side, no, it's not any of them not
Our milk it's not white, no, no our milk is not yours not
Their shadow, no, it's not even the sun, it's not the old sun not
Not, not, not more not, not so much more just not

— But how much blood in the milk!

We've aged centuries beyond here the sound of tortured footsteps
Methods of enforced disappearance, Madres de Plaza de Mayo
Guatemala, El Salvador, beyond here The Philippines, Algeria
Beyond here no grave just the junta – no shame just the police.
Beyond here Palestinian hanging – Bandista, Bandista, Bandista!
Beyond here "ye held up well, dog!" Guilt's just a made-up thing
    anyway

— A fog warning for the entire country!

Here now the sound of wings. Right here. Now gone.
Kasım Alpsoy now here. Kasım Alpsoy now gone.
Cemil Kırbayır now here. Cemil Kırbayır now gone.
Agit Akipa now here. Agit Akipa now gone. Gone. Gone.
So many missing from the roll call – like a mussel suddenly shut.
As if they'd rubbed out what was written – these prohibiting people.

— Aparición con vida de los Detenidos – Desaparecidos!

We never forgot the moment they found the breast. The MOment
    a moTHER nurtures.

Tarih bulsun onları diye diye – köklendik kayada öyle inatçı
Öyle çıplak orta yerde günden geceye ıslak mı ıslak birer fotoğrafla

— Bir oğlağın yaprak kemirdiği hepimizin aklında!

A dropped lawsuit petition, case files covered in dust, overturned
  milk jugs
Buildings entered yet never left, the palace's masked games
Branches entwined in a verdant forest, arms and legs entwined
  in an empty forest
Saying, in order for history to find them – we took root in the
  rock so stubbornly
So naked, standing there day and night clutching these soaking
  wet photographs

— Etched on our memories, a kid goat gnawing on a leaf!

*This poem refers to the 841*st *week of the protests of the
Cumartesi Anneleri/The Saturday Mothers, a group of mothers
who gather in Taksim Sqaure, Istanbul every Saturday morning
to protest the forced disappearance of family/relatives by the
state. See Mustafa Köz's poem 'Firefly'.*

Bizden Önce Biri

Bu düş senin. Bu bitimsiz ova.
Elinden kayıp gideni durdurmak boşlukta.

Sis çanlarıyız. Gecede uyanık.

Gülgillerden Rosa, Kızıl Rosa –
Bir kuş günü kadar kısa.

Günlük işler, eşyalar, kâğıtlar arasında –
Bizden önce biri daha susmuş bu arzuda.

Işığıyla tutuşan ateş böceği. Pervasız neşe.

"Yanı başındayım," diye fısıldıyor Leo.
"Canımın çekirdeği," diyor Rosa *"mein Lieber"*.

Dünya diniyor karda.
Rüzgâr getiriyor ölenlerin sesini.

İçinde neler neler düşünülmüş kaç oda.
Sabah olduğundan habersiz kaç sabah.

Bizden önce biri geçmiş burdan.

Buzdandır zirve Rosa. Yakar. Beden unutmaz –
Kalır bir yerlerde o boşluk tadı.

Sırtüstü uzanırız. Sürer ölümün sarısı.

Someone Before Us

This dream is yours. This never-ending plain.
Whatever slips from your hands sways in this emptiness.

We are fog bells. Awake in the night.

Rosa, of the Family Rosaceae, Red Rosa –
As short as a bird's day.

Among the daily chores and things, among the papers –
Someone before us fell silent in this desire.

A firefly blazing in its own light. A reckless joy.

"I'm right beside you," whispers Leo.
"The core of my being," says Rosa, *"mein Lieber"*.

In the snow the world rests.
The wind bears the voices of the dead.

So many rooms where so much was thought.
So many mornings unaware of themselves.

Someone passed through here before us.

The summit is of ice, Rosa. It burns. The body never forgets –
Somewhere a taste of nothingness remains.

On our backs we lie. As the yellow of death lingers.

Say Ki

Bulanığım hayli. Say ki Thames.
Say ki çıplak bir kadının önünde azalıyor aklım
Say ki koşuyorum lamaların arasında
Say ki gitgide uzadı bacaklarım tarihe dolanmaya
Say ki çapaklı bir dilde konuşur buldum kendimi bu sabah
Say ki kırmızı halıların üzerinde iki sarmal
hangisine düşsem seçemediğim
Say ki aradım seni bir gecenin ortası
daha da yoksunlaşalım mı dedim
daha da korkaklaşalım mı
Say ki herkesler ötekiler oldular birden
Baykuş kılığında geldi bu şiir de

Donu düşük bir sözcüğün
Donunu kaldırmaya uğraştım gün boyu
Pembe ojeli kız ellerini içime soktu
Abartmıyorum
Yalnızlıktan bir dişim daha çıktı
Abartmıyorum
Say ki fırfırlı bir duyguda asılı kaldım

Say ki sahiden beni beni sahiden leylekler getirdi
dünyanın bu ucuna
Say ki yirmisiyle de seviştim arka arkaya
Her şey arkada kaldı
inleyerek ve gerinerek
Bir yolun da karşıdan karşıya geçme hakkı vardı
Say ki dibini boylamış bir resimden yürüdü Ada
sadece onun olan efsunlu kokusuna
Say ki üç kuruşa sattım kendimi o uçuruma

Say It's

I'm murky somewhat. Say it's the Thames.
Say my mind shrivels up before a naked woman
Say I'm darting about among the llamas
Say my legs grew longer to wrap themselves around history
Say I found myself speaking a sleep-encrusted language this morning
Say there are two spirals on the red carpets
I cannot decide which one I should collapse onto
Say I rang you up in the middle of the night
Did I suggest we become more destitute
That we become more cowardly
Say suddenly everyone became the other
And this poem came in the guise of the owl

All day I was trying to pull up the panties
Of a word whose panties had fallen down
A girl with pink-painted nails plunged her hands into me
No exaggeration
Out of loneliness I grew another tooth
No exaggeration
On a frilly feeling I remained suspended

Say the storks really did really did bring me
To this edge of the world
Say I made love to all twenty-one by one
Everything was then left behind
Moaning and stretching out
A road too had the right to cross to the other side
Say Ada walked along a sunken picture
Onto that enchanted scent that belonged to her alone
Say I sold myself to that abyss for a pittance

Say ki omzuna bir kuş, dalgınlığına bir taş sektirmişim
yokluğuna kibritler
Say ki biri ilk defa yürümüş benimle yan yana sonsuza
Ben ona horoz şekeri emen şiirler yazmışım ilk defa
Işıklı bir şeylere benzemişiz giderek
cıvıltılı bir şeylere
Bir rüzgârgülü sonsuz dönmüş ağzımızda
Bir zebra fırlamış benden
İstanbul'a gece uçaktan bakmak gibi olmuşum
alçaldıkça büyüyen ve büyüyen.

Say I skimmed a bird off your shoulder, a stone off your reveries
And matches off your absence,
Say for the first time someone walked side by side with me
To eternity
And for the first time I wrote lollipop-sucking poems for them
Slowly we began to resemble radiant things
Quavering things
A zebra darted out of me
It felt like looking down by night at Istanbul from an airplane
That grew and grew as it descended

About the Translator

Neil P. Doherty is a translator born in Co. Kildare, Ireland, living in Istanbul since 1995 where he teaches at Bilgi University. He is a freelance translator of both Turkish and Irish poetry. In 2017 he edited *Turkish Poetry Today*, which was published in the UK by Red Hand Books. His translations have appeared in *Poetry Wales*, *The Dreaming Machine*, *The Honest Ulsterman*, *Turkish Poetry Today*, *Arter* (İstanbul), *Advaitam Speaks*, *The Seattle Star*, *The Enchanting Verses* and *The Berlin Quarterly*.

www.ingramcontent.com/pod-product-compliance
Lightning Source LLC
Chambersburg PA
CBHW030727150426
42813CB00051B/319